PENGUIN BOOKS
DIME-STORE DAYS

Lester Glassner spent the formative years of his life in upstate New York towns such as
Auburn, Geneva, Lockport, and Syracuse. Born in Buffalo on February 23, 1939, Lester
sought relief from the heavy burden of 1940s reality in haunting the magical worlds of the
five-and-tens and the movie theaters, beginning what was to become a lifelong interest in the
study and collection of artifacts from these two uniquely American art forms. A graduate of
Pratt Institute in 1961, Mr. Glassner is currently employed by CBS Records as picture
editor, designer, and art librarian. He lives with his collection in a small private museum on
Manhattan's Lower East Side.

Brownie Harris, an award-winning photographer of people, places, and things, has worked
for major magazines, newspapers, and corporations. His candid portraits have earned him
one-man shows in Manhattan's leading galleries, and he has an Emmy nomination to his
credit, along with dozens of awards of merit from many important photography associations.
His ability to capture both the capricious and important aspects of his subject matter made
him the perfect collaborator for *Dime-Store Days*. His next major project is a portrait study
of personalities from the world of theater and the arts.

Foreword
by
Quentin
Crisp

Introduction
by
Anita Loos

Design by
Gael Towey Dillon

Penguin Books

DIME-STORE DAYS

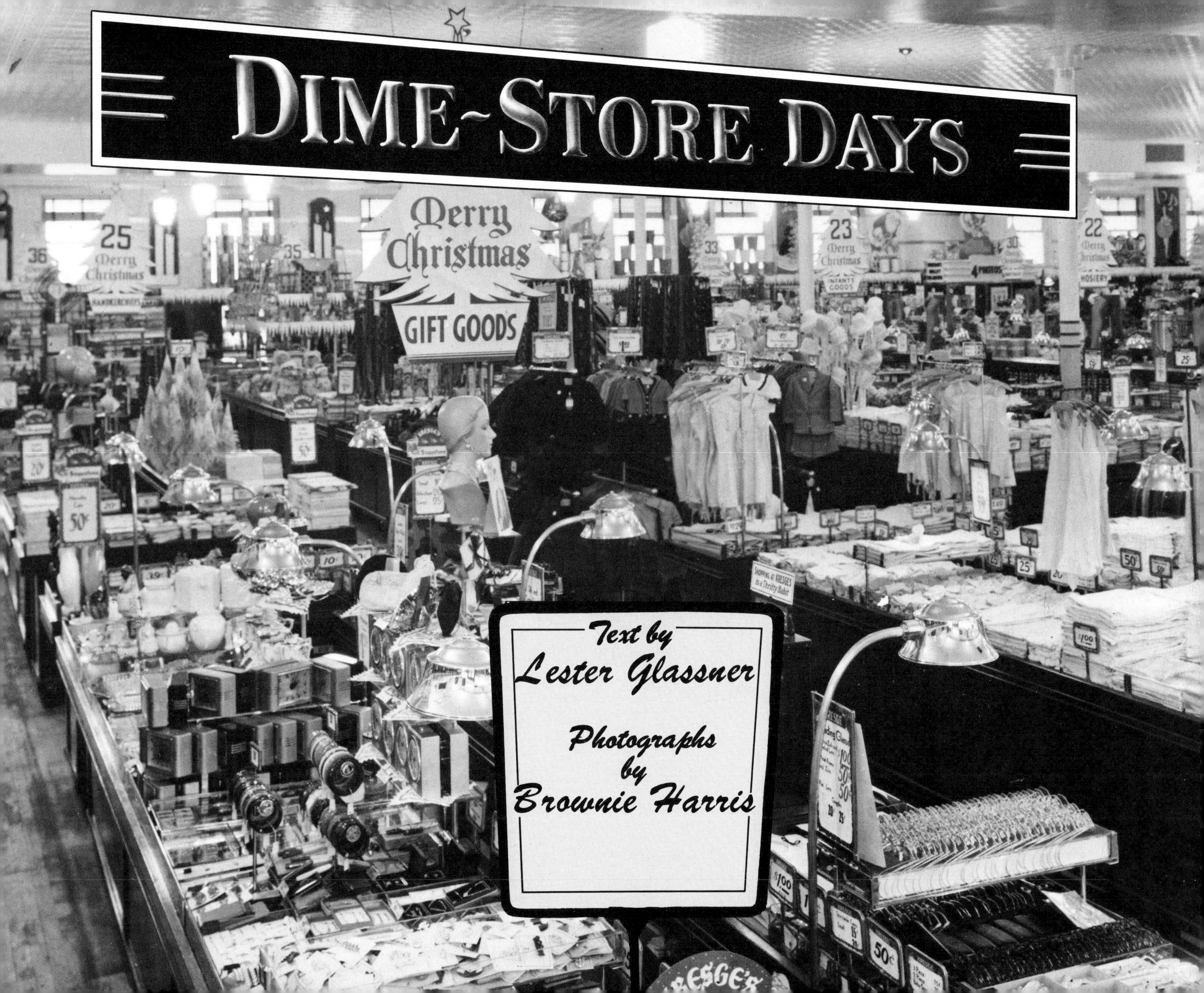

Merry Christmas
GIFT GOODS
25 Merry Christmas
23 Merry Christmas
22 Merry Christmas
HOSIERY
INFANTS' GOODS
SHOPPING AT KRESGE'S is a Thrifty Habit
KRESGE'S

Text by
Lester Glassner

Photographs by
Brownie Harris

Penguin Books Ltd, Harmondsworth,
Middlesex, England
Penguin Books, 625 Madison Avenue,
New York, New York 10022, U.S.A.
Penguin Books Australia Ltd, Ringwood,
Victoria, Australia
Penguin Books Canada Limited, 2801 John Street,
Markham, Ontario, Canada L3R 1B4
Penguin Books (N.Z.) Ltd, 182–190 Wairau Road,
Auckland 10, New Zealand

First published in simultaneous hardcover and
paperback editions by The Viking Press
(A Studio Book) and Penguin Books 1981

Library of Congress Cataloging in Publication Data
Glassner, Lester, 1939–
   Dime-store days.
   1. Variety stores—United States—Collectibles.
2. Moving-picture industry—California—Hollywood—Collectibles.
3. Glassner, Lester, 1939–   —Art collections.
I. Harris, Brownie, 1949–   II. Title.
NK808.G55   1981   745.1'0973   81-767
ISBN 0 14 00.5668 8   AACR2

Printed in Japan by Dai Nippon Printing Co., Ltd., Tokyo
Set in Times Roman and Eterna Light

The best part of a human being is the childhood that remains in us all. And this book will provide everything of childhood that you will ever seek!... Anita Loos

New York, March 4th 1980

To my amazing
and wonderful parents,
who taught me the
language of dreams,
and to
Anita Loos,
whose genius for life
gave me hope

Anita Loos and Lester Glassner, New York City (1980).

DIME-STORE HONOR ROLL

We would like to thank the following people for their invaluable assistance and friendship:

Patty Andrews Weschler
Haig Adishian
Iris Adrian
Richard Ahr
John Anthes
Katherine Aldridge

Eric Benson
Steve & Kate Barth
John Berg
Bob & Rita Brand (Speakeasy, N.Y.C.)
Rosamund Berg
Bob Buecker
Charles Boyer
Rob Biro
Richard Bernstein
Janet Baran
Jim Brown

Fred Coxen
Margaret Coro
Ben Carbonetto
John Cocchi
Leo & Ada Columbus
Henrietta Condak
Steve & Ellen Conley
Arlene Croce
Philip Castanza
Ron Coro
Culver Pictures
Marilyn Cumberland
Mervyn Clay

Diana Custom Photo Laboratories, Inc.:

Vincent Tcholakian, Anahid Markarian
Shari Dickerson
Frank & Shirley Driggs
Eleanor Dushane
Michael Durham

Laurent & Donna Enckel

Jerry Feirman
Pauline Feirman Miller
Angela Francavilla
Jack Field
Mamie Foster
Ira Friedlander

Edward Glass
Judy Glass
The Glassner Girls: Eva, Ruth, Dorothy, Sarah
Judith Glassman
Jake & Dorothy Glassner
Harry & Lena Glassner
Jeffrey Gorney
Michael George
Freda Glassner Honig
Nancy Grossman
William Glassner
Herb Graff
Abraham Glassner
Jonathan & Anna Guss
Morris Greenberg

Nicole Audelain Harris
Will Hopkins
Selden and Evelyn Harris
Betty Hill
Ben M. Hall
Don Hunstein

Dennis Harrison: The Palace Theater, Lockport, N.Y.

Glen Jantzi
Bud Jacobs
Jerry Jarman
Johnny Jupiter (N.Y.C.)
Sally Jones

Eda S. Kenney
Edwin Kennebeck
Kate Kleber
Miles Kreuger
Amanda Kyser

Arlene Ludwig
Mr. & Mrs. Bruce Laughlin
Robert & Bessie Lesses
Richard & Denise Lindner
Ed Lee
Phil LoCasio

Mark Mahall
Lucas Matthiessen
David & Virginia Morison
Anthony Maggiore
Joel Moore
Eduardo Moreno
Dion McGregor
Michael McNeil
Frank Manchel
Tom Morley
Gladys Moore
Jo Mangiaracina
John Millet
Arthur Maillet
Michael Mantel
Mary

Phoebe McGuire Nichols
Milton & Rosemary Neidenberg

The New York Public Library Picture Collection
Fayard & Harold Nicholas

George Ogee

Neal Peters
Alice Pappas
Louis Pappas
Patina (N.Y.C.)
Teddy Perez
Elena Pavlov
Leslie Peller
Dorothy Peterson
Charles R. Penney
Edwin J. Polster
Stephen Paley
Roz Levin Perlmutter

John Remsen
Robert Richards
Ed Rubin
John Robson
Roger Robles
Mark Ricci (The Memory Shop, N.Y.C.)

Daniel Surak
Dr. Peter Saitta
Eileen Schwartz
Kaoru Shinzaki
Clyde Slate
Paul Slaughter
Anita Siegel
Joyce Santiago
Harvey & Sally Slaughter
Sandy Speiser
Paula Scher
David Smith

Rita Sue Siegel
Candy Snyder
Lucy Surak's Variety Store (Shamokin, Pa.)
Bob Scott
Jim Spada
Kay Sussman
Danny Stein
Ricki Sellner
Chris Slavik
Eloise Vega Smith
Eddie Brandt's Saturday Matinee (Los Angeles, Calif.)
Nancy Sureck

Gladys Turner
Paul Trent

Lou Valentino
Judith Villarrubia
Vincent Virga
Pam Vassil
Judy Vitale
Frank Ventrola

Arnold Weissberger, Esq.
Jim Wong
Doug Whitney
Celia Williams
Wide World Photos (Steve Phillips)
Sandra Wilmot

Christopher Young

Olga Zaferatos
George Zeno

Contents

FOREWORD
BY QUENTIN CRISP

*N*ow rich beyond the wildest dreams of income-tax officials, Mr. Glassner never for a moment forgets the privations of the past. His memory dwells lovingly not on the sparseness of those years but on the brittle ornaments with which he desperately tried to decorate them. As Mr. Beardsley reveled in sin, as M. Genet believed in depravity, so Mr. Glassner worshiped tawdriness. He now lives in a house filled to the exclusion of present comfort with relics of plastic hope from the past. In this book he beckons almost without a word, along corridors which are flanked by shelves weighed down with dime-store merchandise.

His favorite period of history was the forties, when death stalked the world and all merriment was like the smile of a skull. The people he adored were the girls who stood behind the counters in those Woolworthless shops which he frequented as a child. In many ways those saleswomen were very similar to the goods they insolently avoided selling, but they were better in that they were bigger. They aped and probably hoped to become the heroines of those movies of which, in that far-off, happier time, you could see six a week—productions so abysmally "B" that only Mr. Glassner can remember which wan wraiths they featured.

Mr. Glassner does not approve of success. The stars we are allowed to recall are not those whom some rich man effortlessly placed upon the summit of fame nor the few who seemed to have drifted upward on wings of spirituality. Here we see only women the marble of whose effigies is streaked with the grime of their past struggles. Of these Miss Crawford was undoubtedly the queen—not because she was elected but because she struck the faces of her competitors with gem-encrusted fists and trampled their falling bodies beneath the leaden platforms of her shoes. She represented perfectly that phase of fashion when women decided to become ogres, her face an icon of ravenous desperation. No amount of lipstick could feed a mouth as hungry as hers; no stockade of eyelashes could provide safety for eyes so terrified; no padding could give the bowed shoulders anything but the boldness of concealed panic.

Those of us who were more or less alive at the time experienced this frantic way of life without a qualm. It is only now, through this strange book, that we look back in amazement at a situation too grim for humor, too shrill for pathos.

INTRODUCTION
BY ANITA LOOS

*W*hen Lester Glassner was a little boy trying to understand the world war in which he was growing up, he stumbled onto an escape from its horrors, degradation, and boredom. He discovered a sort of surcease that could be bought at his own price range, anywhere in town—treasures so colorful that they turned his whole drab life into a world of fantasy.

He spent every free moment wandering through the aisles of the five-and-dime stores, where one could actually reach out and touch a celluloid Charlie Chaplin or thrill to a Kewpie doll that, in his fertile mind, became a living, breathing Jean Harlow.

Added to Lester's dreams were those of millions of other little boys and girls, evoking an adoration so intense that it almost sent up sparks.

Culture, in order to grow, must be fertilized. And it may well be that the glorious trash of the five-and-ten-cent stores played a large part in helping to build the Great American Dream.

REMEMBRANCE

Walt Disney's Three Little Pigs pail, lithographed tin candy container (c. 1934).

*7*his is a remembrance of a childhood that began early in 1939, on the eve of the twilight years of the Golden Age of Style in Entertainment, and coincidentally on the eve of World War II. It was a period in history of the jitters and heebie-jeebies, for a plague of darkness was about to descend on a Depression-weary world. It was a world unknowingly on the brink of losing forever its wonderfully buoyant qualities of youth and innocence, a world coming to grips with some terrifying facts of life: that in order to protect and preserve a bizarre irony known as civilization, a war would have to be fought with a brute force undreamed of a decade earlier.

This heady reality shaped just about every kind of fantasy that passed before the tot's eyes during those years. Looking back on that decade of breezy ironies and stylish fun now conjures up halcyon images of the "stuff that dreams were made of" in a time when we could still afford the luxury of dreaming.

The little boy of that time was profoundly influenced by the "stuff" of this reality: the feverish romanticism and glamour of the movies and the toys that became the physical embodiments of all the shadow-dreams he watched on all the silver screens of whatever flyspeck towns his parents had just moved to. His family moved frequently then, as did most of the population that was seeking war-related employment in the early 1940s. It became an odyssey that enabled him to recognize a kind of continuity to life for the first time: each new town would always have its dreamlands of shows and the five-and-tens. He could survive the constant uprootings by making ritualized pilgrimages to the kindred spirits who dwelled in those extravagant shrines, those special kingdoms that provided both a haven and an education he could never have obtained in any "public school." What more enviable assets could there ever have been for a kid who *willingly* spent his childhood as an "outcast" than those two opulent domains that always satisfied his childish desires for "more"?

This modest visualization is a personally guided reverie through those long-vanished days, which may seem to be as remote as ancient Egypt, but which are, in reality, only yesterday. It is a small but terribly significant part of my life's history, a past that slipped by when I wasn't looking. . . . It's just over there, that second star from the right.

The exuberant and inspiring spirit of my mother, Beatrice, nurtured and shaped dreams that will keep my heart young forever.

*M*ost of the awful truths about the 1940s centered primarily on the war and its aftermath. Here on the home front, however, a kid could remain blissfully ignorant of the facts of life and genocide as they were being played out every day in Europe and Asia.

War toys and war movies blithely offered me the opportunity to play at combat, but I would have none of it. The only facet of the war that I could even dimly perceive, and that I was even remotely interested in, was the constantly whispered secret about the "black market." The very words set off something sinister and awful in my mind, which, at the ages of four and five, seemed to thrive on spooks and phantoms. The obscenities of the war could have turned a more mature heart to stone. Luckily, I came in on it all as one used to come in on the middle of a feature film, with all the subsequent confusions regarding plot and substance. That all of this mayhem suddenly invaded the hallowed shrines of celluloid was an indignity that I would have to endure for the duration.

In that long-ago-and-far-away time before television had begun to wreak its inexorable damage on the human soul, the newsreel was *the* disseminator of bad news, and an entire industry unto itself. How I grew to loathe the hours I was forced to spend watching its murky pornography as it ceaselessly paraded before me (courtesy of Mr. Hearst and his MetroTone News) the loads of death being dropped on Germany and Japan. I began to retreat further and further into my dreams, where there was never a sound of a gun or cannon, or the seemingly endless processions of starving, freezing refugees to remind me that the rest of the world was much worse off than I, who had nothing better to do than crave and demand the insane and glittering surrealism of Technicolored escape—luscious, gaudy, flamboyant musicals, and lavish Walt Disney confections.

Growing up in the movie houses of the war years meant that in addition to being held a mute and captive audience of those dreary newsreels, I also had to suffer through the Previews of Coming Attractions, *Pete Smith Specialties, The Candid Camera, Fitzpatrick's Travelogues, The Three Stooges,* mini-concerts of classical music, quasi-documentaries such as *The March of Time,* filmed War Bond rallies (with hordes of Hollywood celebrities running amok), and last but by no means least, the live onstage appeals for blood donations and scrap. After these the blood *and* bonds *and* scrap could then be bought, donated, or exchanged in the theater lobby, which was suddenly turned from candyland to a displaced bank and/or recruiting office.

After those travesties were over, that other facet of my movie mania would begin. This came in the form of the abysmal lower halves of double features, or "B" movies. "B" signified the creeping paralysis of Poverty Row studio budgets, out of which were created films so understated that they took on a kind of cut-rate poetry, with a language all its own. Most of those little horrors were mercifully free of Major Studio Slickness, and seemed to my unformed mind to mirror—with pinpoint accuracy—the exigencies of survival in a world that had gone berserk with hatred. The sleazy aphorisms of these quickies were geared to the lowest mentalities of that day, but I in my perverse and childish wisdom was able to find constant delight in

The official logo of the New York State Censorship Board.

Opposite page: *Universal Pictures logo (c. mid-1930s). Miniature U.S. fighter plane, glass candy container (c. 1945).*

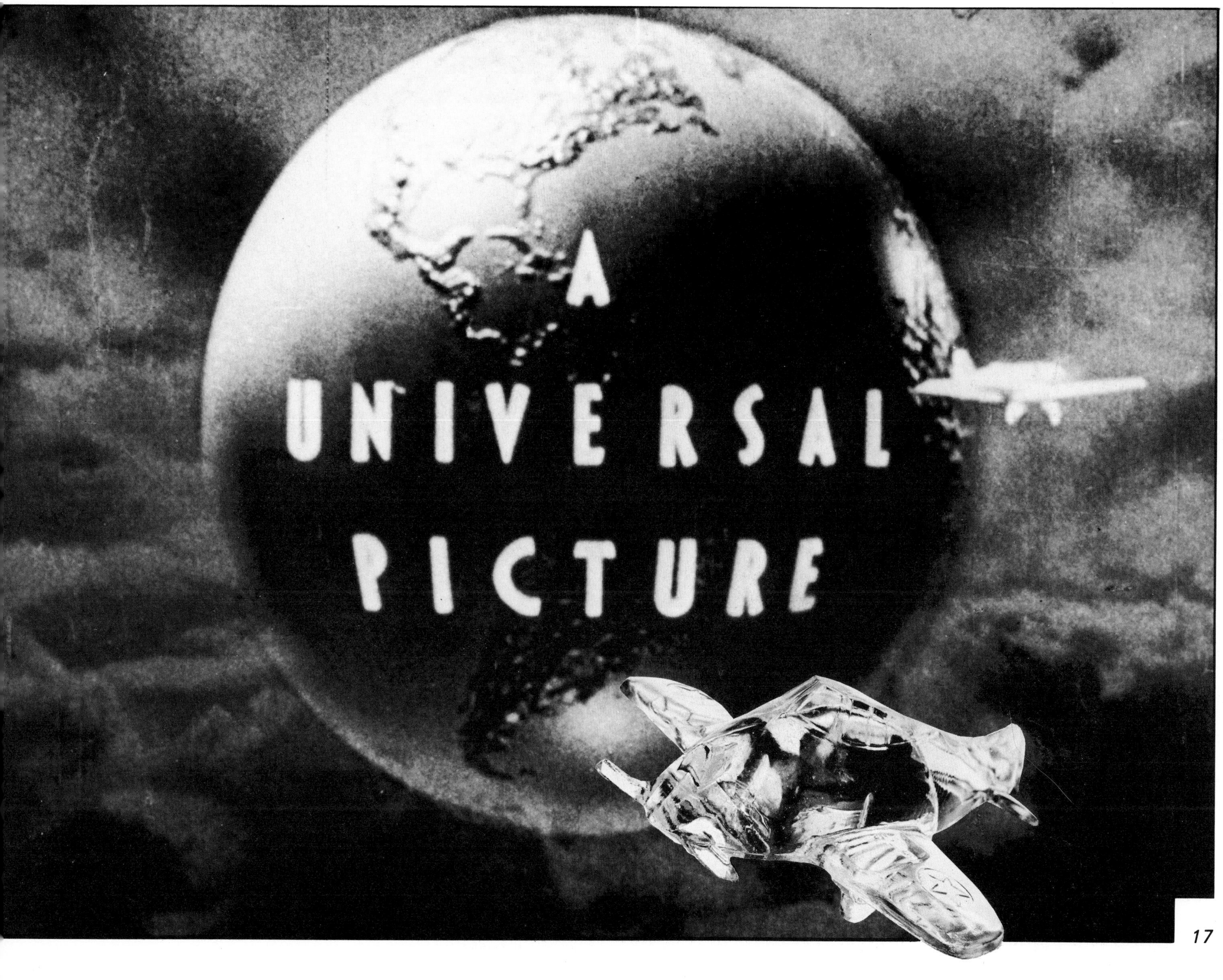
A
UNIVERSAL
PICTURE

The Lester Piano Radio, L. K. Franklin Co., Los Angeles, Calif., bakelite (c. 1938).

watching just how low the producers of these stinkers could sink, just how much they thought they could get away with. Their logos and fanfares usually told the whole story: Lippert, Eagle-Lion, Republic, Monogram, and PRC would invariably elicit a sigh of weary resignation from the other juveniles in the audience, and their post-haste flight up the aisles for more popcorn left me free to soak up the shopworn illusions of the "B's" without any further interference. They were illusions that would ultimately affect my relationship with the world then, and for decades to come.

As I sat there through those halcyon years, in a darkness permeated with the sultry perfume of mentholated raspberry disinfectant and stale popcorn, I was taught the real meaning of life from the likes of Fred Astaire, Walt Disney, Betty Grable, Bette Davis, the Andrews Sisters, and innumerable other deities who collectively manifested an exuberance of showmanship and style that has all but vanished from the face of the earth.

Hollywood films had a wonderfully healthy contempt for reality in those days, which was instrumental in showing me the way over the Rainbow. Once over this Rainbow, it was left to the five-and-tens to help me remain there.

The very existence of the dime store spelled heaven-sent relief from the psychic hardships of childhood in the 1940s. The loss of one's equilibrium from the stony indifference of wartime reality was instantly assuaged upon entering any of those gaudy Xanadus. They were peaceful havens of fantasy and mischief, enchanted Coney Islands where toys, candy, and cosmetics were packaged and sold in the glittering trappings of the Hollywood Style. It was a style that ruled the whole world in that particular decade in every conceivable way, a style that was glamorous, spectacular, and bigger than life.

Kresge, McCrory, Neisner, Newberry, W. T. Grant, and the Mount Olympus of all five-and-tens, Woolworth, mirrored my childhood dream of the universe perfectly, with a kaleidoscope of color and whimsy. It was an endless parade of phosphorescence, of giddy illusions and visual jokes made especially to seduce and satiate the appetites of a child hungry with a passion for caprice and escape. The fun and fancy-free I sought and found without limit in the dime stores began the second the doors swung open. Once past the red-and-yellow enameled scale (Your Wate and Fate 1¢), the perfume of a thousand and one mysteries engulfed me. In those unair-conditioned days the smells of every five-and-ten were far more pungent with character and substance: the oiled bare wood floors, peanuts roasting, potato chips in glass bins warmed to fragrancy by the meager heat of a 100-watt light bulb, the synthetic dextrose of the candy counters (especially the candy corn and the pastilles inside miniature glass telephones), the heavy lusty musk of Blue Waltz perfume, Japanese incense cones, cheap hamburgers frying on griddles that never knew of health laws, cherry phosphates, Skippy Cups, Animal Crackers, cherry Cokes, banana splits . . . all these combined in one stupendous smell that made my senses reel. In the summertime, when the giant floor fans blew, the ambrosial air would be sent into paroxysms of steamy fragrance, cyclones that gusted from one end of the store to the other and back again, creating the 1940s equivalent of "nose candy." Dime stores sold the seasons, and they sold the holidays of all the seasons. I will remember forever how Christmas, Valentine's Day, Easter, and Halloween smelled in the 1940s, with their bizarre candy effigies of symbolic traditions.

This was also the world in which I was introduced to sexuality incarnate—the dime-store dames. These slightly bruised-by-life five-and-ten salesgirls were to me the very essence of Hollywood glamour.

Glass candy container manufactured by the Victory Glass Co. (c. 1946).

There behind each and every counter were the willing and ultimate victims of the Hollywood Style: sinister, luridly cosmeticized concoctions that travestied and actually became road-show versions of Joan Crawford, Rita Hayworth, and Betty Grable. Peroxide-pompadoured, shoulder-padded, sling-pumped, platform-soled, vermilion-nailed, antenna-eyebrowed, gum-snapping, tomato-mouthed, rhinestone-drop-earringed: these macabre daytime shadows gave padded dimension to the movie goddesses that warmed me from the local silver screens. And yet despite their gaucheries, there was something terribly touching about most of them. They were all dressed up with no place to go, except to their stations behind the Woolworth counters of the world.

This was a world in which I became quite adept at seeking out and becoming friends with toys that I knew instinctively could share their secrets with me, secrets which eventually became part of my heart's commands, my very own "Rosebud." Those impish, insolent, and brassy objects of desire that once were visualizations of my heart have now become unforgettable pieces of time, cherished reliquaries from a long-ago series of pilgrimages to my not-so-secret fountain of youth. The selling and packaging of dreams that could be trusted was, once upon a time, a business of serious artifice, an industry whose icons have miraculously endured and have become even more wonderful for that very fact of survival. The giant visual emotions that were the stock in trade of the movies and the five-and-tens represented all of life's popular daydreams, which could be appraised or purchased in a sweetly enchanted domain mercifully removed from war and hate. It was a world where I knew positively that I would never be cheated by life—a place of significant joys, a bewitched playground that kept my life a constant celebration!

Lester Glassner

Behind the counter: Iris Adrian, Hollywood's definitive hard-boiled honey, whose acid wisecracks made her the most durable character actress in the "B" movie world of the 1940s. Seated, Joan Crawford imperiously awaits a black-and-white soda. Above: Soda fountain advertising display (c. 1942).

DISNEYANA

THURSDAY AND FRIDAY

RKO RADIO PICTURES

MICKEY MOUSE VIEWER and WALT DISNEY Film strips In Full Color

Set $3.95 Complete

Includes Mickey Mouse Viewer and 13 Walt Disney Film Strips, comprising condensed versions of famous Disney features.

WALT DISNEY Film strip IN FULL COLOR

© Walt Disney Productions

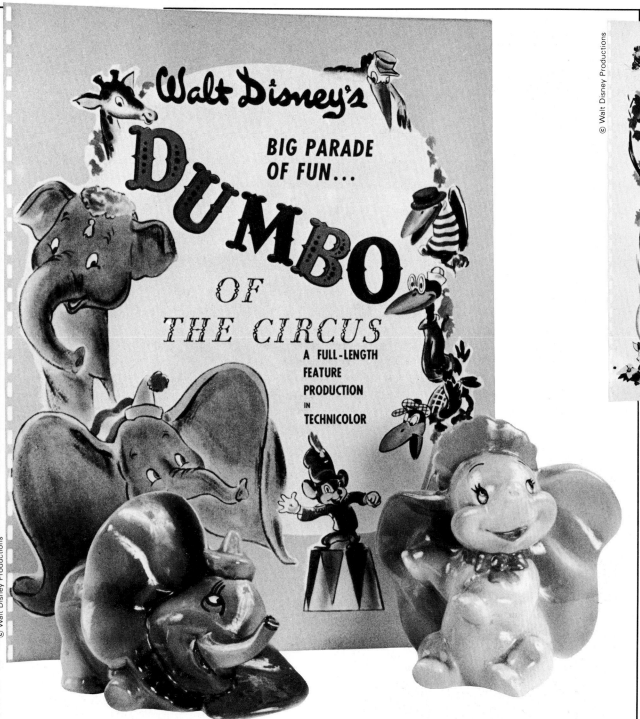

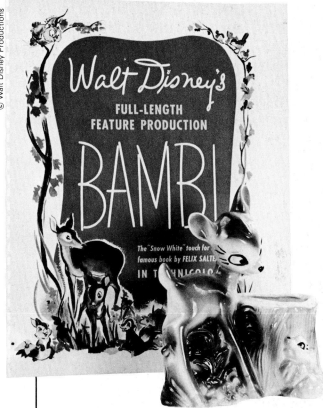

Opposite page: *Previews of coming attractions logo (mid-1940s). RKO Radio Pictures logo. RKO distributed Disney movies throughout the 1940s. This Mickey Mouse Filmstrip Viewer was manufactured by the Craftsmen's Guild of Hollywood (c. 1946).*

Two Walt Disney "friends" from my early childhood: Dumbo ceramic figurines (the Evan K. Shaw Co., 1946). Bambi ceramic planter (Leeds China Co., 1949).

The first movie my mother ever took me to see was Walt Disney's *Snow White and the Seven Dwarfs*. It was an occasion for literally rubbing my eyes in disbelief. I am still not entirely convinced that I have completely recovered from the magical effects of the glowing Technicolor, or the enchanting gentleness of the animation as each scene breathed life into fairy-tale characters that until then I had only seen as flat drawings in the pages of my storybooks. It was an experience of powerful beauty, with a bewitching message of consolation and hope. Every other Walt Disney animated movie that I was taken to see had the same magical effect on me.

The Palace Theater in Lockport, New York, where I first saw all of the Walt Disney masterpieces; Dopey bank (Crown Toy Manufacturing Co., Inc.; composition, c. 1938); Sleepy Valentine (the Paper Novelty Manufacturing Co., c. 1940); and Adriana Caselotti, the voice of Snow White, "wearing" a Snow White paper-doll dress (c. 1938).

Left to right: *Seven Dwarf dolls, molded felt bodies, hand-painted faces, made in England (c. 1938); Snow White statuette, amusement-park prize, plaster (c. 1938).* Background: Movie Mirror *magazine cover (c. 1938).* Foreground center: *Big Little version of the Disney film containing black-and-white line illustrations of the story done by the Disney Studio (c. 1938).*

Walt Disney's

FULL LENGTH FEATURE PRODUCTION

Pinocchio

IN MULTIPLANE TECHNICOLOR

Distributed by RKO Radio Pictures Inc.

JIMINY CRICKET— What a Show!

Pinocchio was a wonderful surprise package of a movie—a shower of shimmering stardust hurled at me by the breathtaking magic of Walt Disney's brilliant animators. Each of my countless childhood viewings of this extravagantly and lyrically Technicolored spectacle filled me with instant and undying rapture.

Left to right, *all c. 1940: Jiminy Cricket bank, composition; theater lobby poster; Pinocchio salt shaker, ceramic.*

Children's storybook (movie version) illustration.

Walt Disney's **Pinocchio**

DOLL CUT OUTS

Pinocchio doll, composition, movable arms and legs; Pinocchio pull toy—Pinocchio strikes the bell as the donkey is pulled across a surface— lithographed paper laminated to wood, metal bell and wheel axis (Fisher-Price Toy). Extra-large-format Pinocchio paper-doll cutout book.

WALT DISNEY'S **PINOCCHIO**

Donald Duck and Panchito, pressed wood fiber, mounted on slotted wood base (c. 1945); Joe Carioca dancing windup doll, composition, French (c. 1947); The Three Caballeros *theater lobby poster* (c. 1945); Joe Carioca watch, Ingersoll (c. 1948).

Saludos Amigos *record-album cover* (c. 1944); Donald Duck ceramic figurine (c. 1947); Joe Carioca bookend, pressed wood fiber (c. 1945);

*W*alt Disney's *Saludos Amigos* and *The Three Caballeros* were two birthday moviegoing experiences given to me by my parents in February of 1943 and 1945. The star of both films was Joe Carioca, a parrot whose comic tempestuousness seemed to have been modeled very clearly after the famous Brazilian bombshell Carmen Miranda. The tropic Technicolored heat of these animated features and the fiery, pounding samba rhythms of their musical scores were completely unlike anything I had ever seen or heard before.

WALT DISNEY'S
miracle musical FEATURE
The **Three**
Caballeros
in Technicolor

featuring
PANCHITO
JOE CARIOCA
DONALD DUCK
and in the flesh
AURORA MIRANDA of Brazil
CARMEN MOLINA of Mexico
DORA LUZ of Mexico

RELEASED THROUGH RKO RADIO PICTURES, INC.

© Walt Disney Productions

© Walt Disney Productions

© Walt Disney Productions

29

*C*armen Miranda often got dressed up like a dancing strawberry-banana split, and when she did, there was just no stopping her. Her enormous influence on the artificial-fruit industry made the kitchens and dining rooms of my childhood resemble orchards of wax, plaster, and paper ornamentation.

Fruit basket decal (c. 1945). Superimposed are, clockwise from left, grapes, a plaster wall plaque, an apple, a plum, an orange, and a banana, wax (c. 1946).

30

Banana and mixed fruit, plaster wall plaques (c. 1945). Below: Hat or dress ornaments. Czechoslovakian. Glazed fabric (c. mid-1930s).

A DREAM OF VICTORY

Ceramic planter (c. 1941).

Commemorative patriotic pin, metal (c. 1942).

The Japanese sneak attack on Pearl Harbor, December 7, 1941, not only sank a significant portion of our pitifully small navy, but also set off an explosion among American souvenir manufacturers. The propagandizing of just about everything that could be bought or sold became a giant industry during the early years of the war, and the dime store sold the best of those icons of patriotic hope.

REMEMBER PEARL HARBOR 12-7-41

Save waste fats for explosives

...KE THEM TO YOUR MEAT DEALER

TOKIO EXPRESS

PRODUCTION MEANS VICTORY
Let's give it a "Lift"
LIFT
GLOBE HOIST COMPANY
DES MOINES, IOWA · PHILADELPHIA, PA.

Wartime conservation poster (c. 1943).

With women participating heavily in the fight for Victory, Hollywood stars had a field day exploiting their dime-store charms as singing and dancing riveters and torpedo jockeys. Far left: *Diana Lynn on a mission for democracy.* Below: *Betty Jane Rhodes as a warbling welder in Priorities of 1942* helped Paramount Pictures win the war. Serving for Victory meant that even telephone operators could now be as stylishly important as military personnel, and they were given the star treatment on, of all places, matchbook covers.

SERVING FOR VICTORY

SHE DOESN'T WEAR A UNIFORM BUT IS IN THE THICK OF WAR ACTIVITY HANDLING CALLS THAT SPEED THE NATION'S DRIVE TO VICTORY

CLOSE COVER BEFORE STRIKING

SO WE'LL MEET AGAIN

BUY MORE WAR BONDS

PRAISE THE LORD, AND PASS THE AMMUNITION!

Morale-boosting postcards, greeting cards, and movie-star coloring books helped sell millions of dollars' worth of defense bonds.

Ann Sheridan PAINT BOOK
AUTHORIZED EDITION

For Victory
BUY UNITED STATES WAR SAVINGS BONDS and STAMPS

"Bonds buy bullets," Ann tells the people.

The bond drive goes over the top!

Patriotic but pretty: Cosmetics packaged in military trappings made life on the munitions assembly line a bit more chic and glamorous. Even the ubiquitous cherry pin of the 1940s went patriotic, mirroring the hues of "Old Glory."

Flirting for Victory: Dona Drake (Paramount Pictures), wearing an Uncle Sam pin, adorns a New Year's greeting from Hollywood. Patriotic funeral parlor souvenir fan, cardboard with wooden handle (c. 1943). Costume jewelry flag pin, metal (c. 1943).

V-mail, special priority mail to and from personnel of our armed forces outside the continental U.S., gets the seal of approval from Ann Miller. Pulp magazines exploited the bitter loneliness of wives, fiancées, and sweethearts left behind to wait till the boys came home.

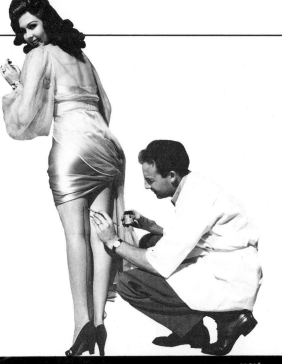

"Bottled Stockings" were one way of solving the nylon shortage. Lucky and clever Ann Miller had her own makeup man to paint a seam up the back of her formidable gams. Rita Hayworth, pinup of a million military wet dreams, was the ultimate of everything that was dreamlike, escapist, and larger than life. This magazine cover promoted her latest luscious Technicolored eyeful, Cover Girl (Columbia, 1944). Chalk figurine (c. 1942). Patriotic lapel pin, bakelite and rhinestones (c. 1942).

"PIC"

SHOW BIZ
GOES TO WAR
By Abel Green

RITA HAYWORTH

AUGUST 29, 1944
PRICE TEN CENTS
TWELVE CENTS IN CANADA

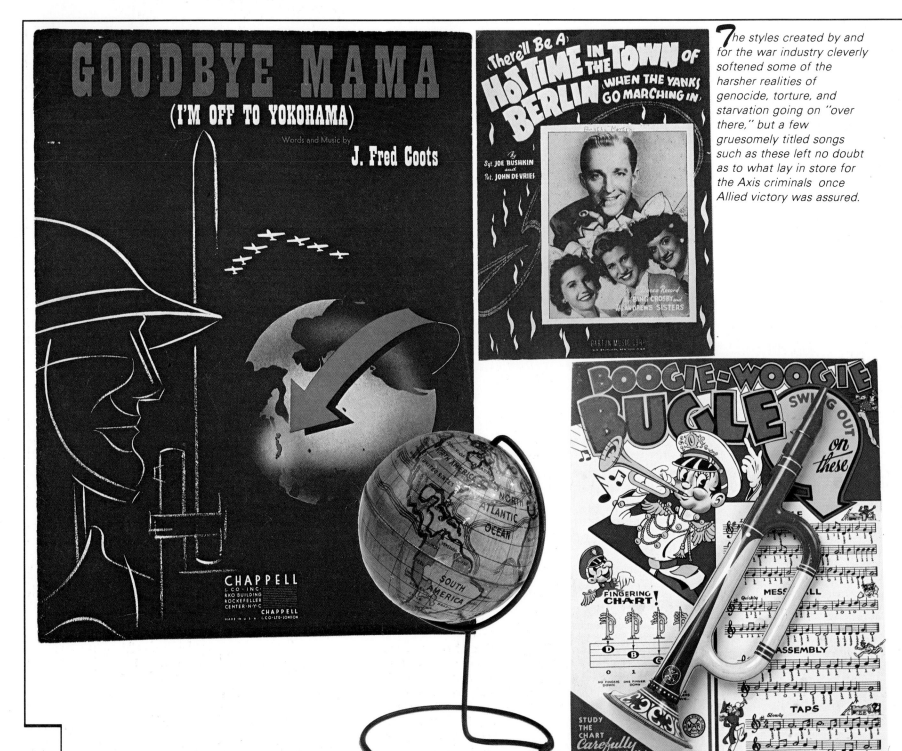

The styles created by and for the war industry cleverly softened some of the harsher realities of genocide, torture, and starvation going on "over there," but a few gruesomely titled songs such as these left no doubt as to what lay in store for the Axis criminals once Allied victory was assured.

753 HOLLYWOOD CANTEEN, HOLLYWOOD, CALIFORNIA

MODERN SCREEN

JULY Still 10 CENTS

CLARK GABLE

SCREEN GUIDE December, 1943

15c

EXTRA! COLOR PHOTOS SINATRA AND TAYLOR!

MEET JOHN GARFIELD— "THE LITTLE GIANT!"

MOVIE-RADIO

TEN CENTS • CANADA 15c

Exclusive! Truth About Stars And the Draft

SCREEN ROMANCES

"WINGED VICTORY" THE ARMY AIR FORCES HIT FILM starring LON McCALLISTER

15c

6th WAR LOAN BONDS YOUR THEATRE

LON McCALLISTER JEANNE CRAIN

tion Picture MAGAZINE

HOLLYWOOD'S MOST EXCITING NEW PERSONALITY GUY MADISON—A Profile by Sidney Skolsky

Movieland

AUGUST 15¢

TE WITH FLYNN? Errol's own story, as never before revealed

More than two million servicemen passed through the doors of the Hollywood Canteen from the time it was opened by Bette Davis in October 1942. With the magical names and faces of Clark Gable, Tyrone Power, and Jimmy Stewart off in the thick of combat, Hollywood was forced to spawn some not-so-magical replacement heartthrobs. Left: Lon McAllister, Guy Madison, and the peerlessly incompetent Sonny Tufts.

39

First Sensational Behind-the-Scenes Drama of That Seductive Jap Siren of the Airwaves!

"TOKYO ROSE"

A windup doll, celluloid (c. 1946).

Tokyo Rose—Iva Ikuko d'Aquino, born in the United States on July 4, 1916—had become, by the end of the war, infamous enough for immortalization in a Hollywood "B" movie. The purring voice of this comic-strip evil seductress, one of many ladies broadcasting from Japan, urged thousands of GIs across the Pacific to stop fighting because their sweethearts back home had all jilted them, they were losing the war, and it would be a lot easier to surrender to Tojo.

JAM YOUR CIGARETTE BUTTS ON THIS RAT

Propaganda ashtray, glass (1943).

A commemorative stamp observing the 50th anniversary of the birth of the movies. In a remote South Pacific jungle, GIs are about to watch some morale-boosting Hollywood-style entertainment on a sheet hung between two palm trees. The stamp has been hand-canceled at the Hollywood Station post office (c. 1944). Charging tin infantryman (c. 1941). Scottie dog pin, celluloid (c. 1941). This defense bond recruiting poster was pictured in a movie fan magazine advertisement (c. 1944).

PATRIOTIC THEATRES DISPLAY THIS POSTER

Make your local movie house your easy, convenient headquarters for the purchase of war stamps and bonds. Night and day, day and night, the motion picture theatres of America are ready to serve you.

15,000 theatres are united in this great campaign under the sponsorship of the Theatre Divi-
War Activities Committee of the Motion Picture Industry, 1501 Broadway, N. Y. C. ★

*E*xposing the horrors of totalitarian regimes gave Hollywood "B"-movie producers a golden opportunity to exploit sex and violence. Above: For the crime of refusing to join the Nazi Youth Movement, Bonita Granville is publicly flogged; Hitler's Children, RKO Radio (1943). Right: When Men Are Beasts *was pure Poverty Row, with an all-no-star cast,* Exploitation Pictures (c. 1944).

A war-weary public lined up outside of newsreel theaters all over America just to make sure that it was really true; Guild Theater, New York City (c. 1945). Ads for *Victory Newsreels,* The Buffalo Evening News (1945). The Hotel Berlin *advertisement for a film depicting the collapse of the Nazi regime;* Warner Brothers (1945). 35mm slides of significant battles in the fight for Victory (c. 1946).

Opposite page: Hitler's Madman, *the story of the extermination of the Czech village of Lidice;* Ava Gardner (extreme left) *being menaced by John Carradine as the notorious Heydrich;* M.G.M. (1943). War tank glass candy container, Victory Glass Co. (c. 1945). This patriotic lapel pin is a souvenir of my uncle Jake's hitch in the U.S. Navy.

ANIMATED ROMANCE

I'M UP IN THE AIR ABOUT YOU SWEETHEART!

February 14 was always a special day for my schoolmates and me. Valentines such as the ones pictured below were the vehicles of innocent flirtation. All cards are made of lithographed paper.

Moon, German (c. 1935).

Old Mammy read
in my palm last night,
That you'll be my Valentine
Is she right?

Negro valentine, animated (c. 1935).

Cat valentine, animated (c. 1932).

Fold-out umbrella (c. 1935).

To My Valentine
I'm blowing up

Sodas, German (1923).

What shall I do Ain't your umbrella built for two!

45

The Andrews Sisters—Patty, Maxene, and LaVerne—filled the dark years of World War II with the sunshine of their fresh and novel harmony. They were a home-front national treasure whose sizzling boogie-woogie and rumba rhythms gave the 1940s a background sound, a zingy vitality that poured out in seemingly endless profusion from thousands of rainbow-hued jukeboxes, radios, movie theaters, record stores, nightclubs, and U.S.O. canteens. The brash and beguiling optimism of these three charming girls boosted the morale of our soldiers throughout the war.

Opposite page: *A typical wartime movie and stage show headlining a personal appearance by the Andrews Sisters, Paramount Theater, New York City (c. 1942). This page: Theater lobby poster, Universal (1945). Song sheet covers that sold over a million copies each: "Rum and Coca Cola" (1944); "Pennsylvania Polka" (c. 1942); "Hold Tight—Hold Tight" (c. 1939).*

In the Navy, *Universal,* *(1941).* Upper right: *Entertaining homecoming GIs on a New York City pier (c. 1945).* Lower right: *Decca records publicity photographs (c. 1944).* Opposite page, left to right: *Swingtime Johnnie,* theater lobby poster, *Universal Pictures (1944);* an Andrews Sisters record brush, lithographed tin handle attached to cotton cleaning brush base *(c. 1945);* a *Decca 78 r.p.m. phonograph record, shellac (c. 1943).* Maxene, Patty, and LaVerne in their first—and phenomenally successful—movie musical, Buck Privates, *Universal (1941).*

48

In the year 1975 a dime-store dreamer's "dream of a lifetime" finally came true. I met *them* during the Broadway run of their hit 1940s-style musical, *Over Here*. The gift of Patty Andrews' dressing-room chair from *Over Here* made the author grin with extrasensory anticipation, even way back in 1945.

THE ANDREWS SISTERS in *Swingtime Johnny*

with

HARRIET HILLIARD
PETER COOKSON   MATT WILLIS
BILL PHILLIPS   TIM RYAN

and

MITCH AYRES
and His Orchestra

THE ANDREWS SISTERS in OVER HERE!

THE ANDREWS SISTERS
DECCA RECORDS
North Side Music Shop
59 West 34th Street
Wabash 4621

DECCA

ANY BONDS TODAY?
(Irving Berlin)
ANDREWS SISTERS
With Vic Schoen And His Orchestra
4044

PATTY

GLORIOUS GLASS

The inexpensive manufacturing technique of mass-producing glassware, known as machine-molding, once made the futuristic shapes of Art Deco available to dime-store shoppers all across America.

Bird vase, made in England (early 1930s). Vase (c. 1940). Sugar and creamer set, "Moderne Art" pattern, Indiana Glass Co. (c. 1931).

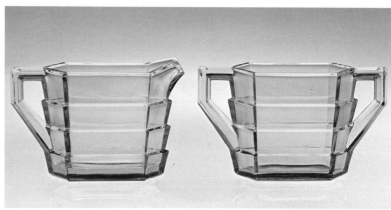

Vases (late 1930s).
Sealtest Dairy
Company cottage
cheese container that
doubled as a beverage
glass; this is one of a
series that featured
Walt Disney
characters (c. 1939).

ALL STAR PARADE

MICKEY

Left to right: *Ribbed pitcher and sailboat orange-juice glass set, Hazel Atlas Glass Co. (c. 1938). Relish-dispensing set with glass serving spoons, chrome lids, and wooden knobs (c. 1940). Orange-juice reamers, Hazel Atlas Glass Co. (c. 1940). Cobalt glass bank (c. mid-1930s).*

Juice glasses
with concentric
banded
"Rainbow"
pattern
(c. 1940).

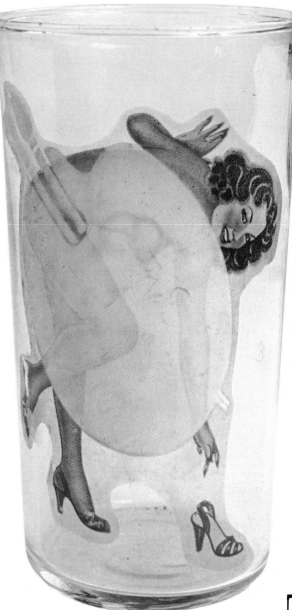

Novelty water glass.
When it is filled with
water, an illusion of
impudent nudity is
produced (c. 1941).

DIME-STORE DAMES

Blue Waltz perfume was a custom blend of oriental decadence and exotic artificiality.

BLUE WALTZ
PERFUME
DISTR. NEW YORK
5/8 FL. OZ.
MADE IN U.S.A.

*S*eductive eyes, larcenous hearts, and smoldering promises promote the very latest in lip allure. Dime-store chic was a style invented by Hollywood for twelve-o'clock girls in nine-o'clock towns. Hollywood's alliance with the five-and-tens of America made glamour affordable to star-struck shopgirls and schoolgirls. Cosmetics that were supposedly used in the dream factories made most of the women I saw as a child look like streetwalker versions of Veronica Lake, Lana Turner, Betty Grable, and Barbara Stanwyck.

The absolute ultimate of dime-store chic, Marion Martin (*opposite page*), seared her brassy image into the minds of a generation of "B"-moviegoers in the 1930s and 1940s. Listening to her inimitable delivery of hard-boiled dialogue, many women became convinced that she used all of the beauty aids pictured here.

BE IRRESISTIBLE TONIGHT WITH IRRESISTIBLE PERFUME

Irresistible

𝒴OU picture the Irresistible woman before you see her. She appears in a halo of exquisite fragrance. Men are instinctively drawn to her. The power to attract, to fascinate is the secret of IRRESISTIBLE PERFUME. Let it be yours, too.

On your next adventure apply a touch of Irresistible Perfume to your hair, on your lips, your throat and behind your ears. A drop, too, on your lingerie is so feminine and so exciting.

Millions of women everywhere — on Park Avenue, along Broadway, in countries throughout the world . . . prefer IRRESISTIBLE PERFUME for its exotic, lasting fragrance.

To be completely ravishing use all of the Irresistible Beauty Aids. Each has some spe-

YOUR LIPS INVI-   LIPSTICK

Lipstick cartridge containing four shades, metal (c. 1941).

Compact containing rouge, powder, and lipstick, chrome-plated tin (c. 1940).

Adele Jergens, before she became queen of the "B"s at Columbia Pictures. Here she is modeling in, of all places, a pulp confession magazine (c. 1943). Underneath that gleaming wave of hair on the side of her head lies concealed a "rat," an indispensable component used by those practitioners of the rolled and coiled hairstyles that were widely popular throughout the 1940s.

"Rats" came in various sizes and colors, this being the smallest version; cotton (c. mid-1940s).

ASS'TD INVISIBLE HAIR PINS MADE IN U.S.A.

#712 *Lorraine* HAIR ROLL   HARRY GLEMBY, INC.   5¢

With her classy dime-store face and figure, Ann Savage was the kind of tough tomato that lusting GIs once referred to as "a real hunk of femininity." Her hair alone was worth a million "hubba-hubbas."

SMOKE HAZE

Tintex
SMOKE HAZE
STOCKING DYE

For
NYLON
RAYON
COTTON
LISLE
SILK
WOOL
NO BOILING NECESSARY

GIVES NEW, FASHIONABLE COLOR-BEAUTY TO FADED HOSIERY. SMARTEST SHADES EASY!...QUICK!

PARK & TILFORD PRODUCT

SANITARY
KID HAIR
CURLERS
OMY SIZE 39¢

CONTAINS MARLES ★ ADDS COLOR AND LUSTRE

LOVALON
Hair Rinse

CONTAINS
6
RINSES   #12 HENNA

MADE WITH U.S. GOVERNMENT CERTIFIED COLORS

SAN FRANCISCO • CALIF.

LOVALON WHICH TYPE ARE YOU?

Veronica Lake
CAMEO SKIN TYPE
Use Flesh or Natural

Paulette Goddard
IVORY SKIN TYPE
Use Rachel or Flesh

Lana Turner
HONEY SKIN TYPE
Use Rachel or Windsor Rose

Dorothy Lamour
TROPIC SKIN TYPE
Use Brunette or Sun Peach

Laraine Day
AMERICAN BEAUTY BLEND
Use Windsor Rose or Champagne Rachel

WOODBURY
SHADES
dr   our type

39¢

WOODBURY
NEW COLOR CONTROLLED SHADES

Sunglasses from the 1940s, with their khaki-green- and/or sepia-tinted lenses, were designed to complement perfectly the furious reds of lipstick and rouge worn by Technicolored stars such as Betty Grable. Left: Mutoscope pinup cards could be purchased in amusement park penny arcades during the 1940s.

IS MY FACE RED?

Ella Raines, a floozy for all seasons, vamping famous fall-guy Elisha Cook, Jr., in the Universal Pictures mystery thriller *Phantom Lady* (1944). In Ella's line of screen work, all of the products pictured here could have been of great assistance in staving off the withering hand of time.

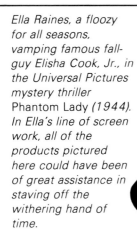

CHENYU
Cloudsilk
MAKEUP

TANGEE
FACE POWDER

FLESH

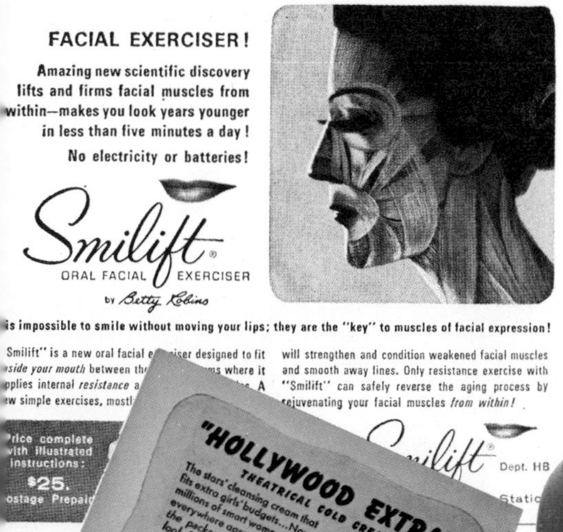

*L*yda Roberti, a vamp from the halcyon days of early Hollywood talkies, set the style for dime-store seduction with blindingly platinum hair and a rhinestone personality to match. Clock compact, pressed tin (c. 1941). Costume jewelry, rhinestone pins (c. late 1930s).

The fanciful influences of Carmen Miranda on the 1940s costume jewelry industry produced earrings, necklaces, and pins of visionary wit. Carmen "wears" (top necklace) glass cubes hung from a chain of celluloid; (bottom necklace) celluloid cherries hanging from a celluloid chain. (both c. 1940). Below: pin, bakelite (c. 1939). Above: Earrings, enamel and wood (c. 1939). Banana earrings, glazed ceramic (c. 1941).

Screen streetwalkers and their empty
promises abounded in the films of the 1940s,
and their influence could be found in many
of the artifacts sold in the five-and-ten.
These were for the dime-store
boudoir on the
wrong side of the
tracks.

*A Noritake
figurine
of gracious
and enduring
charm (c. 1938)*

*A
souvenir
miniature
shoe
(c. 1947).*

*Pressed-glass
perfume
bottle
(c. 1932)*

Left to right: *Wooden hat stand (c. 1930). Portable celluloid vanity kit, ideal for short trips on the Greyhound bus (c. 1935). Plaster wall plaque (c. 1944).*

Crawford-inspired regalia: bracelet, metal (c. 1947); purse, lucite (c. 1947); hand-beaded shoe, leather (c. late 1940s); A Woman's Face, coming-attractions slide (1941); magazine (c. 1930).

A 1932 publicity portrait for Rain (United Artists). Joan with her first husband, Douglas Fairbanks, Jr., on an unsuccessful "second honeymoon" trip (1932). On May 13, 1933, she filed suit for an interlocutory decree of divorce.

To Aster from Joan Crawford

During the dreaming years of my childhood, Joan Crawford movies were object lessons in how to survive the dreary days of postwar reality. Watching her as she cunningly used her flawless romantic glamour and shoulder-padded courage to wage war against an army of cads, cheats, and weaklings convinced me that her spirit was forged in fire.

Grim and unremitting as was her ankle-strapped determination, it was her face that spoke the most eloquently to me: the exquisitely sculpted cheekbones, the astonished expressiveness of her eyes, and her mouth, which had all the dramatic mystery and excitement of a secret military target. All of these comprised a facade of exalted beauty and sublime visual poetry, a glowing essence of Hollywood stylishness.

See JOAN CRAWFORD in
"HOLLYWOOD CANTEEN"
A Warner Bros. picture

"It really tastes best!"
says

JOAN CRAWFORD

Lovely Joan spreads Christmas cheer,
Enough to last the whole New Year!
And for a toast to old St. Nick—
Note: Royal Crown Cola is her pick!

When Joan took the famed taste-test
Royal Crown Cola tasted best!
P. S. All you lads and lasses:
Five cents gives you two full glasses!

"WHEN YOU SAY MERRY CHRISTMAS,"

says Joan, "make it mean
more this year than ever
before. Say it with *more* U. S.
War Bonds for your friends,
your family, and yourself!"

Joan Crawford

TAKE TIME OUT FOR A "QUICK-UP" WITH

ROYAL CROWN COLA

BEST BY TASTE-TEST

66

Joan Crawford

Heeding the old adage, "out of sight, out of mind," few actresses would have the courage to stay off the screen for more than a year, as Joan has done. Her last picture, "Above Suspicion," was made at M-G-M early in 1943. Shortly after, she left Metro to sign a contract with Warner Bros., and has held out all these months until she found a picture that she considered right for her. It will be "Mildred Pearce," in the making at the time you read this.

19

Pre-promotional fan magazine publicity for her "comeback" film, Mildred Pierce (c. 1944). In this December 1944 magazine advertisement, Joan promoted her appearance in the Warner Brothers all-star, flag-waving entertainment, Hollywood Canteen, sold defense bonds, spread Christmas cheer, and extolled the efficacy of Royal Crown Cola.

The kind of Woman most men want — BUT SHOULDN'T HAVE! That's...

Mildred Pierce

JOAN **CRAWFORD**
JACK **CARSON**
ZACHARY **SCOTT**

Presented by

WARNER BROS.

WARNER BROS. PICTURES

Joan Crawford was triumphant after her blighted stardom was restored by her 1945 Oscar-winning performance as the grimly self-sacrificing Mildred Pierce. Theater lobby poster (1945). Joan holding "Oscar." Warner Brothers publicity still (1945).

Joan and her daughter Christina, whom she adopted in May 1940; publicity photo (c. 1946). Below: Christina's adoptive brother, Christopher, helping Mommie fix her makeup (c. late 1940s). Center: *Dressed to kill: the famous "Crawford Look"* (c. 1945). Opposite page: *Columbia Pictures publicity still* (c. 1943). *Silver Screen,* movie fan magazine (c. 1936). Joan was never without several hundred pairs of "Gypsy" brand false eyelashes. These were purchased at the auction of her personal effects in New York City in January 1978.

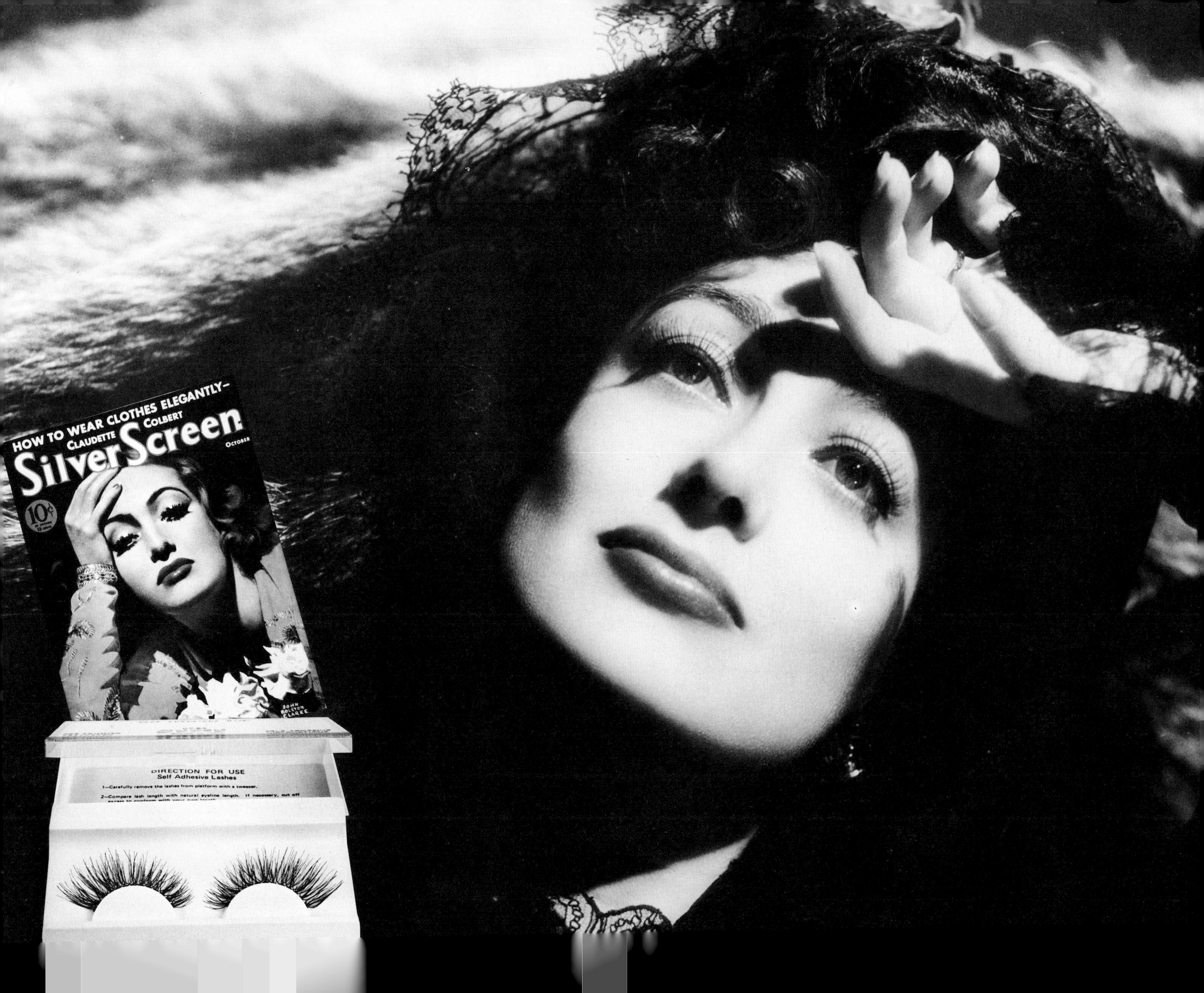

DIRECTION FOR USE
Self Adhesive Lashes

1—Carefully remove the lashes from platform with a tweezer.

2—Compare lash length with natural eyeline length. If necessary, cut off excess to conform with your own length.

THE REAL McCoy: McCoy Pottery

Birdbath

*T*hese are more examples of fruit-and-flower configurations that were inspired by Carmen Miranda. All were produced in the 1940s and are made of machine-molded ceramic.

Pomegranate.

Lily-flower vase.

Flower vase.

A-bunch-of-bananas cookie jar.

SALT & PEPPER SOUVENIRS

Left: *When the plungers are pressed, salt and/or pepper is released from the bottom of the glass containers (c. 1930).*
Below: *Salt and pepper are contained in cylinders that connect clear lucite bands (c. 1946).*

These three pairs of bakelite dispensers were manufactured between 1937 and 1940. They reflect the classic Art Deco style.

pepper pepper pepper pepper

pepper pepper pepper pepper

salt salt salt salt

salt salt salt salt salt salt salt salt salt

salt

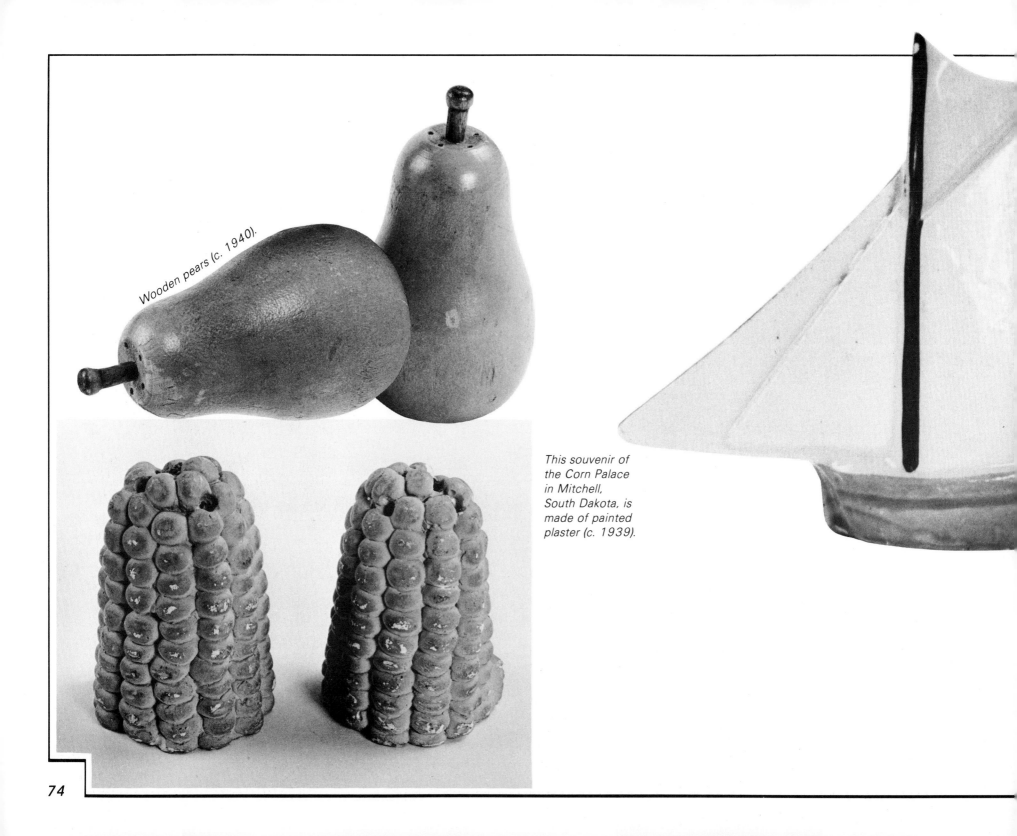

Wooden pears (c. 1940).

This souvenir of the Corn Palace in Mitchell, South Dakota, is made of painted plaster (c. 1939).

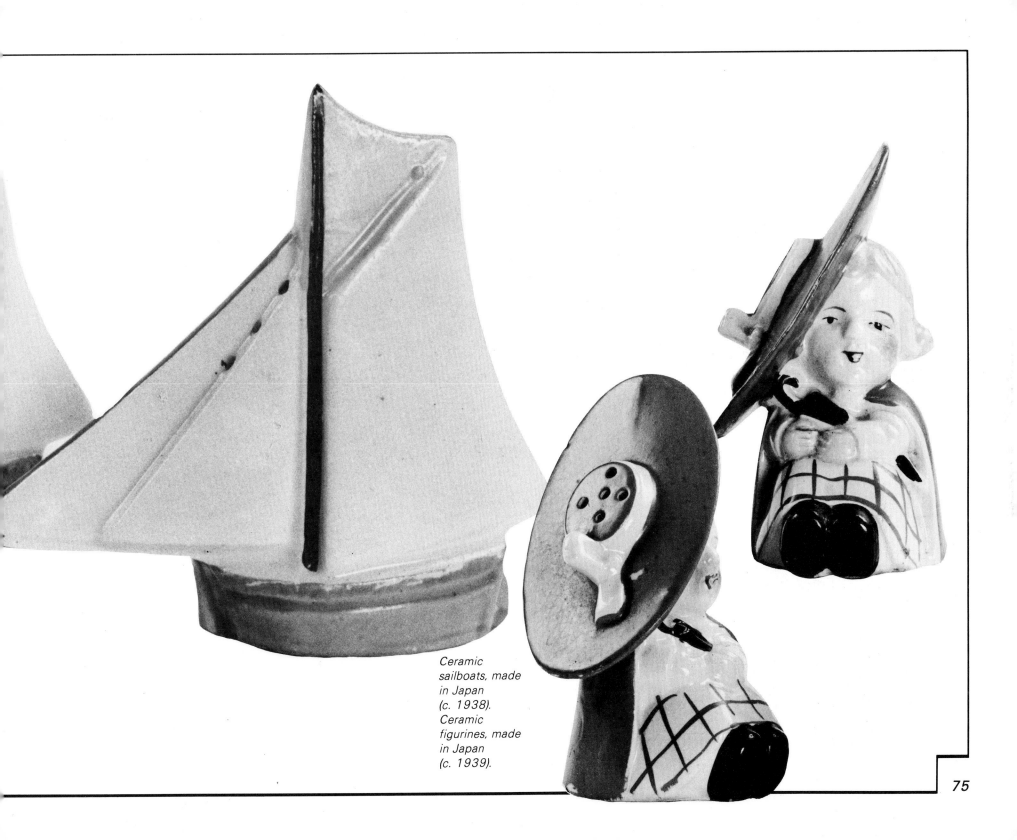

Ceramic
sailboats, made
in Japan
(c. 1938).
Ceramic
figurines, made
in Japan
(c. 1939).

Walt Disney's Three Little Pigs playing cards (c. 1933). The Big Bad Wolf cup and saucer, the Salem China Co., Salem, Ohio (c. 1934); pig in cup, pottery bank (c. late 1930s). Three Little Pigs figurine set, made in Japan, bisque (c. 1934).

WALT DISNEY'S SILLY SYMPHONY "Three Little Pigs" PLAYING CARDS

BY SPECIAL PERMISSION WALT DISNEY ENTERPRISES

THREE LITTLE PIGS.

© Walt Disney Productions

© Walt Disney Productions

Sleeping-piggy bank, made in Germany, bisque (c. late 1920s). Another version of the fiddling pig, from Walt Disney's "Silly Symphony," The Three Little Pigs; made in Japan, ceramic (c. 1934).

WOODEN WISEGUY

*M*ae West with Charlie in a publicity photograph from their infamous December 1937 NBC radio broadcast. Promotional "giveaway" souvenir doll with movable mouth and eyes, the New York World's Fair, cardboard (1939). Charlie McCarthy Fan Club membership button, lithographed tin (1939). Opposite page: Paper-doll cutout book with movable mouthpiece (c. 1939). Charlie McCarthy Halloween masquerade costume (c. 1940). Get-well card (c. 1939).

CHARLIE McCARTHY
LICENSED BY EDGAR BERGEN

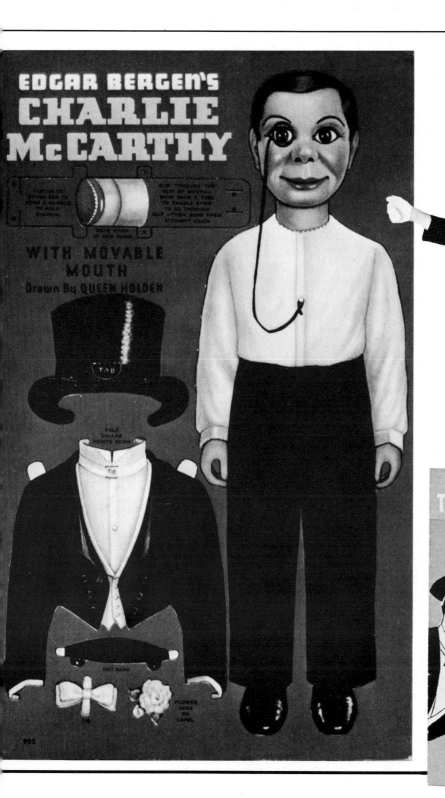

EDGAR BERGEN'S CHARLIE McCARTHY

WITH MOVABLE MOUTH

Drawn By QUEEN HOLDEN

$\mathcal{C}$harlie McCarthy, the legendary ventriloquist's dummy who was always dressed like the patron saint of sophistication, was one of the most bizarre icons of my childhood. He was "operated" by an adult of incisive and unremitting vapidity by the name of Edgar Bergen. Charlie's outspoken and monocled mock haughtiness, working against Bergen's bumbling diffusiveness, resulted in stylish and whimsical routines that kept their appeal fresh and undimmed for decades. They also inspired some of the most beautifully animated character toys ever made in America.

It sort of knocked me
OFF MY FEET
to hear
that you are sick —
ty quick.

HERE'S CHARLIE McCARTHY
TO HELP YOU GET WELL!

IF YOU WERE ILL WOULD YOU TAKE OUT HEALTH INSURANCE TO PAY FOR A NURSE?

TURN HERE

OH DEFINITELY! THEN I'D TAKE OUT THE NURSE!

Left to right: *Figurine, plaster (c. 1940). Storybook, illustrated with photographs (c. 1939). Card game with McCarthy wisecracks printed on the back of each card (c. 1940).*

EDGAR BERGEN'S

CHARLIE McCARTHY

Rummy CARD GAME

A Day With CHARLIE McCARTHY

Souvenir giveaway spoon (c. 1939).

*T*here was no thrill quite so wonderful as listening to the "Charlie McCarthy Radio Show" on a radio designed specifically for that purpose. The author, wearing his Charlie McCarthy Halloween costume, continues to enjoy that comforting listening ritual by the magical process of autobiography.

Radio, bakelite (c. 1939); Halloween costume: molded felt top hat, starched gauze mask, cotton tuxedo. The tin lapel button designates lifetime membership in Charlie's Fan Club (c. 1940).

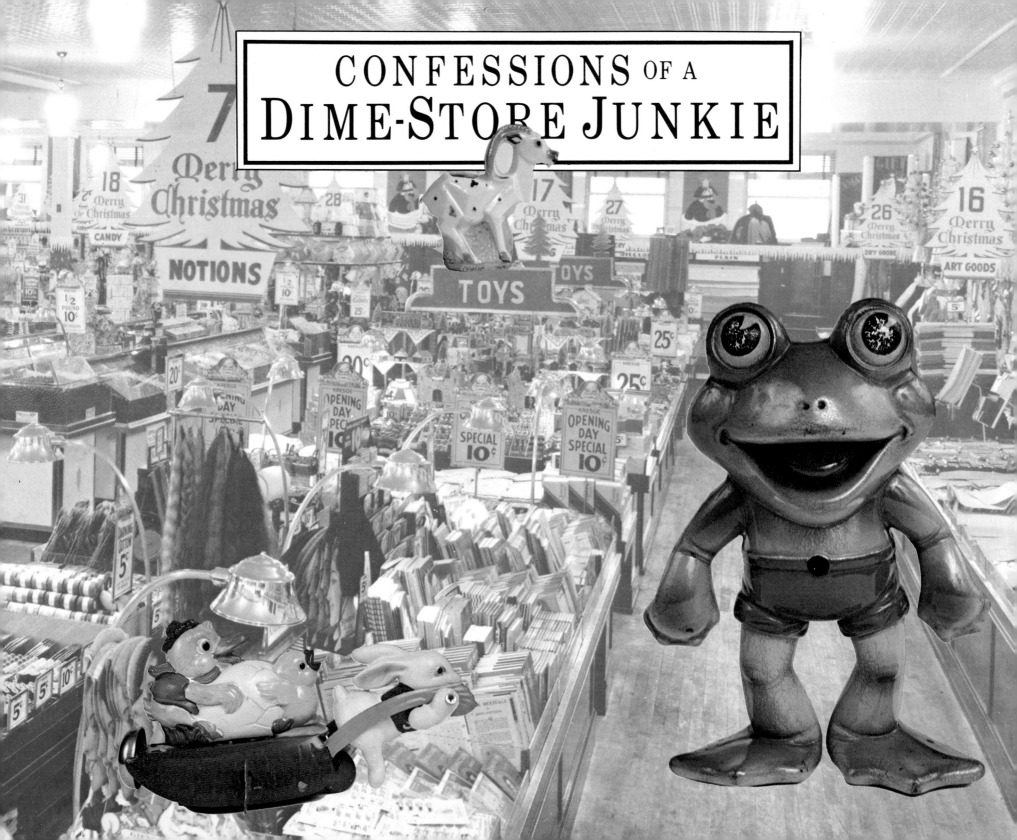

CONFESSIONS OF A
DIME-STORE JUNKIE

Opposite page: *A five-and-ten interior (c. 1940); Easter windup toy, celluloid (c. 1945); ram figurine, ceramic (c. 1940); frog squeeze toy, rubber (c. 1949). Below: The author seated on a wood "delivery boy" pull toy. When pulled across a surface, the boy's head swings from side to side as his legs pedal the wheels, American (c. 1935). Inside the cart are celluloid cherry hat ornaments, Czechoslovakian (c. 1930).*

*T*he astonishing sorcery of the five-and-ten helped conquer the cold and dreary world of adult austerity. With seductively reflective surfaces as its most alluring attraction, the dime store was a garden of delights, providing a lost child with a cozy asylum of tranquility and joy.

Glass telephone candy container with detachable (wood) receiver, American, Victory Glass Co. (c. 1945).

*I*n the 1940s, Ringling Brothers, Barnum & Bailey had nothing on the star-spangled circus parade that the five-and-ten put on all year long.

Background: *Detail of tin top (c. 1947). Leading the parade: George the Drummer Boy, Louis Marx, lithographed tin with spring action motor (c. 1946); celluloid elephant with glass bead eyes; elephant bank, chalk (c. mid-1940s); monkey, cardboard head, movable wooden limbs covered with real fur (c. late 1930)s; drum majorette, chalk statuette.*

Left to right: *Clown salt shaker, made in prewar Japan (c. 1940); clown windup toy, celluloid head, tin body containing spring mechanism; bareback rider, celluoid, movable limbs (c. late 1930s). Background: cardboard picture puzzle (c. 1946).*

*N*o American Dream has ever been complete without the comforting and comical images of man's "best friends." The five-and-ten has always supplied the most thoroughly whimsical of these, although I, personally, have never been able to find any endearing qualities about mice—excluding, of course, the incomparable charisma of Mickey.

Left to right: *Doll holding slate, celluloid (c. 1939); animated radio valentine (c. mid-1930s); dog salt shaker, ceramic (c. 1940); cat bank, ceramic (c. 1939); Mickey Mouse lamp, chalk (c. 1936); Felix the Cat doll, pressed wood fiber (c. 1935); mouse on scooter, wood with jointed limbs (c. 1940); dog statuette, plaster (c. 1945).*

CEILING PRICE

39¢

Storks, pelicans, palm trees, and gardenias brought an exotic and aquatic Floridian paradise to gritty small-town America.

Background: *"Wall mural" decals or, as they were once called, "transfers."* Left to right: *Celluloid storks were designed to decorate a baby's room (c. 1940); a roly-poly bird dressed in the latest Harlem fashions, celluloid (c. early 1930s); a bird in a bonnet and a gardenia, plaster wall plaques (c. early 1940s); cruise-ship salt and pepper shakers, ceramic (c. 1940); a man overboard, a celluloid doll in distress (c. 1940).*

The classic and traditional American confrontation was between cowboys and Indians. Translated into witty configurations of the dime-store style, these strangely dignified and exotic effigies told another kind of story to my innocent heart.

Indian fold-out valentine (c. 1940); seated Indian, celluloid (c. 1938). Three Indians, two canoes, celluloid (c. 1940).

SAY YOU'LL BE MINE

90

Crouching cowboy with gun, a tin noisemaker (c. 1948); Lone Ranger Big Little Book (c. 1939); cowgirl figurine, chalk (c. 1940); kiddie cowboy doll, celluloid (c. 1940); traffic-cop doll with animated hand, celluloid (c. 1940); toy truck, painted metal (c. late 1930s).

Left to right: *Impish innocence: seated in back of a truck, the author, age 7; dolls: girl with bonnet, boy in pajamas, celluloid (c. 1940); seated figurine pincushion, porcelain (c. late 1930s), headband holds a cushion for pins and needles; girl in bloomers, painted gesso on composition (c. early 1930s). Background: Romping children; fragment of candy promotion display (c. mid-1930s).*

92

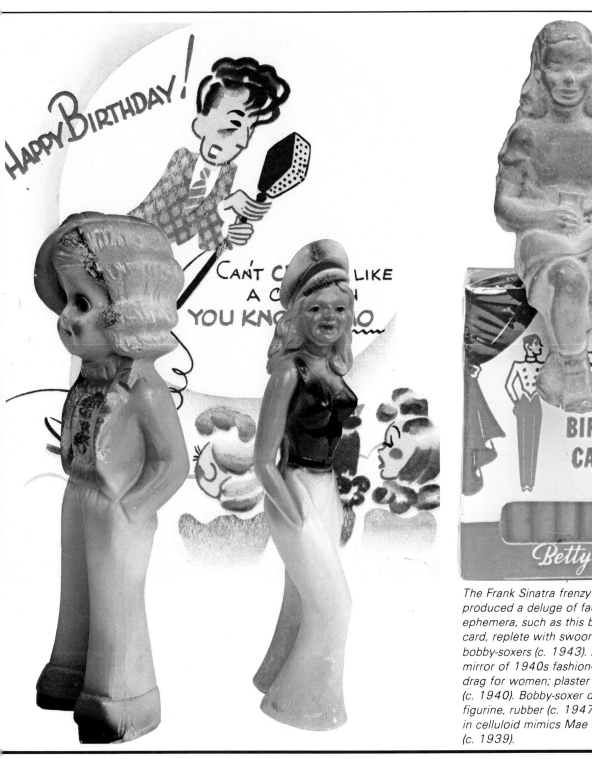

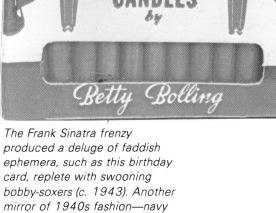

Provocatively posed for action, these slightly corrupt-looking miniaturizations mirrored Hollywood's tarts, floozies, and gold diggers with five-and-ten accuracy.

Women in pants personified a fashion craze introduced by 1930s Hollywood that was carried to ultimate perfection by the street punks of 1940s Harlem; plaster figurine (c. 1937).

The Frank Sinatra frenzy produced a deluge of faddish ephemera, such as this birthday card, replete with swooning bobby-soxers (c. 1943). Another mirror of 1940s fashion—navy drag for women; plaster (c. 1940). Bobby-soxer dollhouse figurine, rubber (c. 1947). A siren in celluloid mimics Mae West (c. 1939).

BLACK MAGIC

The black images of my childhood did not come from actual experience with black children but from the commonplace objects I saw around me. The universal and unquestioning acceptance of those objects by both black *and* white adults helped to perpetuate racial stereotypes.

The tap-dancing Nicholas Brothers had a style that seemed like pure improvisation. The dazzling face of Lena Horne on the cover of a popular magazine. An incense burner of the period, bisque (1930).

To Our Good Friend "Lester" Take It Easy and Be Happy Nicholas Brothers Harold & Fayard 4-3-75

CHOO CHOO

SUNDAY NEWS
NEW YORK'S PICTURE NEWSPAPER
November 14,

J. EDGAR HOOVER on DEATH IN HEADLINES

August 13, 1938

Collier's

5¢ A COPY

BEN JORJ HARRIS.

9/9/45

Dear My Pal Jeffrey:

TWICE THE GOOD WISHES

TWICE THE GOOD FUN

AND twice as long   TILL ANOTHER ONE

JENNY AND BENNY
ANOTHER "NIFTY" TOY
REG. U.S. PAT. OFF.

NO. 751/122

Left to right: *The cover of a nationally circulated magazine (1938); figurine with basket, ceramic (c. 1939); birthday card (c. 1945); Jenny and Benny windup toy, celluloid doll seated on a wooden donkey with a spring-action motor concealed in its stomach (c. 1939).*

The Adventures of
LITTLE BLACK SAMBO

FINDS POT
ADVANCE 2

SEES TIGERS
FIGHTING AROUND
TREE • BACK 1

MEETS 4TH TIGER LOSES
UMBRELLA • BACK 1

TALKS WITH FRIENDLY
MONKEY • ADVANCE 2

CHASES PLAYFUL
BUTTERFLY
ADVANCE 1

FINDS TIGERS
MELTED TO BUTTER
ADVANCE 1

HEARS TIGERS
GROWL • BACK 1

MEETS 3RD TIGER LOSES
PURPLE SHOES • BACK 1

MEETS FRIENDLY
PARROT • ADVANCE 2

MEETS 1ST TIGER LOSES
RED COAT • BACK 1

PUTS ON CLOTHES
BACK 1

MEETS 2ND TIGER
BLUE TROUSERS

CARRIES POT OF BUTTER
HOME • ADVANCE 1

The FINISH

SAMBO
5

There was never any time more wonderful than when my mother read Little Black Sambo to me as only she could. This legendary storybook also took the form of games like this beautifully illustrated example (1945). Butterfly McQueen was another of Hollywood's famous stereotypes. Her Minnie Mouse voice and expertise at faking dim-wittedness kept her career afloat from the late 1930s to the onset of the civil rights movement. Opposite page: Smiling servitude, 1940s style: left to right: a maid holding a soft-boiled-egg timer, ceramic and glass (c. late 1930s); Porter orange-crate label, paper on wood (c. late 1930s); windup railroad porter, celluloid (c. 1946); Mammy Memo reminder pad holder, paper and plastic (c. late 1940s); Hattie McDaniel graciously accepts a drink from her boss in a recently discovered outtake from Gone with the Wind.

LITTLE BLACK SAMBO

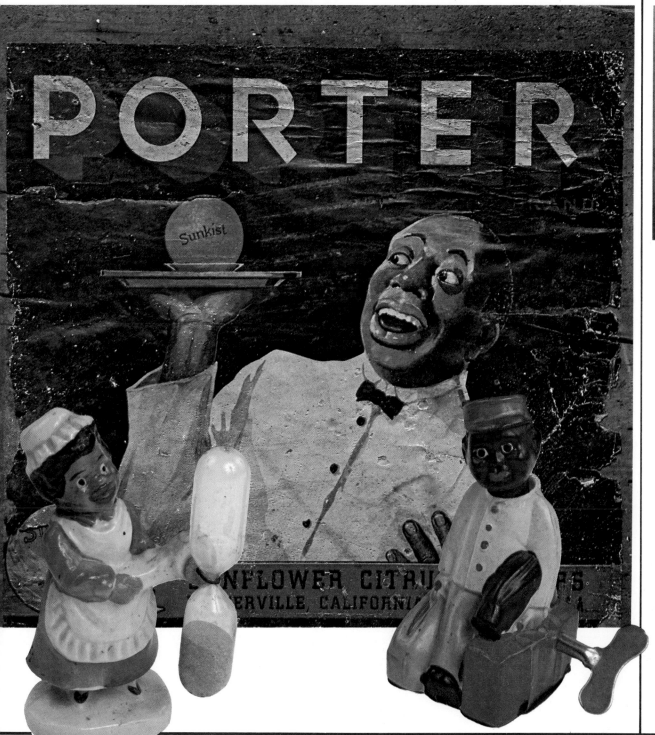

TINSEL TIME:XMAS*

A white Christmas in wartime America was an occasion of incalculable poignancy, mitigated only by the dazzling ornaments of hope sold in the dime stores. It was the most festive holiday of them all, in a time when death and destruction were daily facts of life.

Wandering the aisles of the five-and-ten during this season of optimism and consolation was cause for rejoicing in all of the tender and joyous qualities of humanity. It was also a welcome opportunity to revel in a carnival of unparalleled brilliance, mirrored by tinsel and the hypnotic radiance of bubbling Christmas tree lights.

"Christmas" was rarely spelled out in the dime stores of the 1940s. "Xmas" was the abbreviation used in displays and advertising, and I will always associate the term with the Christmases of my childhood.

Gift tag, paper (1940).

Keep it dark until Dec. 25TH

Bubble lights: plastic, glass, and Freon (c. 1947).

Electric wreath, cellophane and cardboard (c. 1947).

Pressed-paper Santa
candy package
(c. 1948). Christmas
card printed in metallic
silver ink (c. 1940).
Celluloid reindeer
(c. 1945). Holly sprig
were used for gift-
wrapping decorations,
gesso on paper
(c. 1940).

MERRY CHRISTMAS

Left to right: *Foldout paper Santa table-top or under-tree decoration, Germany (c. 1930). Roly-poly Santa, celluloid (c. 1940). Santa head, wall display decoration, gesso on composition, 14" × 24" (c. 1930).*

Comic-strip heroes
were participants in
Yuletide celebrations
throughout the
1940s; greeting card
(c. 1945). Santa in
sleigh, celluloid (c.
1948). Pressed-paper
candy cylinder.

101

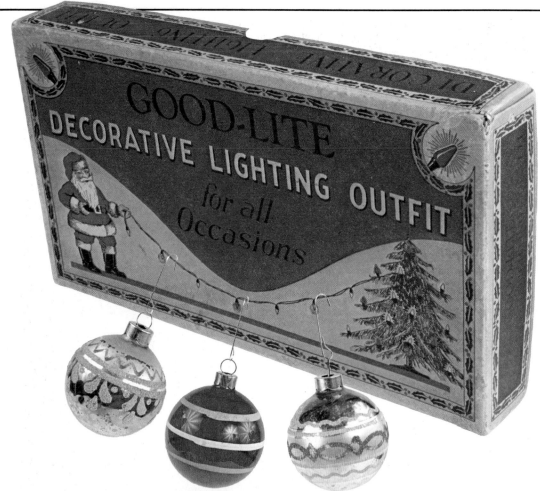

Xmas tree light package; calendar cover; glass ornaments, German (c. 1930); Santa bank, plaster (c. 1948), Santa and reindeer Christmas card, German (early 1900s); paper houses placed under an Xmas tree display or with an electric train set, German (early 1930s); Santa on the roof, velour-covered wire, papier-mâché head, hands, and feet (c. 1920s).

103

SPOOKS & PHANTOMS: HALLOWEEN

*H*alloween, with its witches, fiends, hags, and demons, fed my perpetual desire to be terrified by apparitions and spooks. My make-believe world of childhood found no greater source of raw material than the dime-store effigies and disguises of a prankster's holiday.

Left to right: *Paper mask and cardboard nose painted with gesso, Germany (c. 1930). Cardboard pumpkins (c. 1945). Painted gauze masks (c. 1945). Pumpkin party favor with whistle mouthpiece. The paper coil unfurls when air is blown through the mouthpiece, enameled wood (c. 1940).*

*O*wning a toy 16mm movie projector with its very own toy films made a movie-crazy kid of the 1940s his own theater manager and projectionist. Mickey Mouse cartoons and *Our Gang* comedies were a luxury no dime-store dreamer could afford to be without. Hand-held or tabletop movie frame viewers were also available for kids on fixed allowances.

—catalog—

STARTING SUNDAY MAY 3, 1970

THE DAVID WEISZ CO.

presents a

public auction

OF THE COUNTLESS TREASURES ACQUIRED FROM

ARS GRATIA ARTIS

TRADE

Metro Goldwyn

STAR

20th CENTURY FOX

MEMORABILIA

PUBLIC AUCTION
FEBRUARY 25-28

SOTHEBY-PARKE-BERNET LOS ANGELES

Opposite page: *The ruined dreams of a fairy-tale kingdom—a false-fronted Main Street silently ponders its fate on what was once M.G.M.'s largest outdoor sound stage (c. 1977). The official catalogs of two major-movie-studio auctions of obsolete costumes and props (c. 1970–71). Left: Here is that shudder-producing Paramount Newsreel logo, a visual voice of doom that sent me dashing up the aisle to the comfort of the candy counter or the bathroom. Bottom left: Edward Small Productions logo. Mr. Small was a prominent manufacturer of "B" movies for the discriminating moviegoer of the 1940s.*

PARAMOUNT NEWS

HOLLYWOOD
MADE IN HOLLYWOOD
MOVIE-VUER

WHAT A THRILL MOVIES

With 1 Movie subject

"EXCEL MOVIES"

16 mm

HAL ROACH
'OUR GANG' COMEDY

MICKEY MOUSE
FILMS

WALT DISNEY'S MICKEY MOUSE
& SILLY SYMPHONY CARTOONS

EDWARD SMALL
PRODUCTIONS

This is a classic example of the second- and third-run movie theaters that proliferated in the small-town neighborhoods where I grew up. Dreamland usherettes represented the lavish style of the downtown movie palaces, where I could be admitted only if I was accompanied by one or both of my parents. The Whistling Movie Toy. Air blown through the mouthpiece propels the illustrated paper cards, creating an optical illusion of a dancing minstrel (c. 1939). The Movie Game, during the course of which the winner acquires valuable Hollywood celebrity real estate (c. 1925)

Jujubes, made by the Heidi candy company, tasted like the essence of phosphorescent 20th Century-Fox Technicolor. No trip to the movies was ever complete without consuming several boxes. Hollywood Bowl souvenir, rubber (c. 1935). A 1940s-style candy vending machine reflecting Betty Grable's sweetly reassuring smile (c. 1943).

CUT-OUT DOLLS
CARMEN MIRANDA
Authorized Edition

𝒞armen Miranda in motion—accompanied by the torrid sambas of her Banda da Lua and supported by her legendary nine-inch platform-soled shoes—undulated and slithered her bare-midriffed personality across acres of glassy bakelite floors in a succession of luridly Technicolored musicals in the early 1940s. From her cavernous maroon mouth issued a florid torrent of sounds, a convulsive gibberish of fractured English and Portuguese, mirroring in gaudiness the tutti-frutti salad of junk jewelry that adorned every available square inch of her diminutive anatomy. Rolling her insinuating eyes and gesticulating madly with fingertips that appeared to have been dipped in blood, she surpassed Hollywood's wildest dreams of itself with her flamboyance and comic sensuality.

Carmen Miranda cutout dolls, paper (c. 1943). Record album holding three 78 r.p.m. shellac records (c. 1941).

111

Exactly one month before I was born, this radiant portrait of Bette Davis appeared on the cover of Life magazine. A few years later, by the time I had begun to understand such things, Miss Davis had become the ultimate million-dollar baby in a five-and-ten-cent store by being enshrined in a paper-doll cutout book. She was also seen on the cover of the theme-song sheet music of one of her greatest movie hits of the 1940s, Now, Voyager.

Bette's Own Clothes

Bette Davis PAPER DOLLS
Costumes from her Screen Plays
Doll 1
THE BRIDE CAME C.O.D. · IN THIS OUR LIFE · THE MAN WHO CAME TO DINNER · AND OTHER PICTURES

IT CAN'T BE WRONG
Lyric by KIM GANNON · Music by MAX STEINER

WARNER BROS. PRESENT
BETTE DAVIS
PAUL HENREID
in
Now, Voyager

movie MIRROR
OCTOBER
10¢
Taylor's Real Life Story
MAN FIND ROMANCE AT LAST?

LIFE
BETTE DAVIS
JANUARY 23, 1939   10 CENTS

Photograph by Alfred Eisenstaedt

Life magazine, copyright 1939 Time Inc.

The Rialto Theater in Lockport, N.Y., showed an endless succession of double features of the very best "B" movies of the 1940s. An "A" fantasy like The Wizard of Oz was also featured from time to time. The Rialto was a monument to the kind of failed style I loved so well. Song sheet cover (1939). Judy Garland, Bert Lahr, Ray Bolger, and Jack Haley. Above marquee: Menacing Margaret Hamilton as the Wicked Witch of the West.

THE GLORIOUS ASTAIRE: FRED ASTAIRE

Top Hat *advertising press book with pop-up cover. Fred's top hat unfolds and flips up as the cover is opened (1935). Opposite page: The logo for previews of coming attractions (1945). Fred Astaire publicity photographs for the film* Top Hat *(1935).*

*O*f all the sublimely escapist visions that fed my hungry eyes during the dreamy decade of the 1940s, none surpassed the vision of the dream embodied by the magical personality of Fred Astaire. The wit and emotional expressiveness of his genius made him, in my eyes, a prince of an enchanted domain, a land of enthralling reveries and ethereal elegance where my heart could always find its ultimate dream of exalted and romantic perfection.

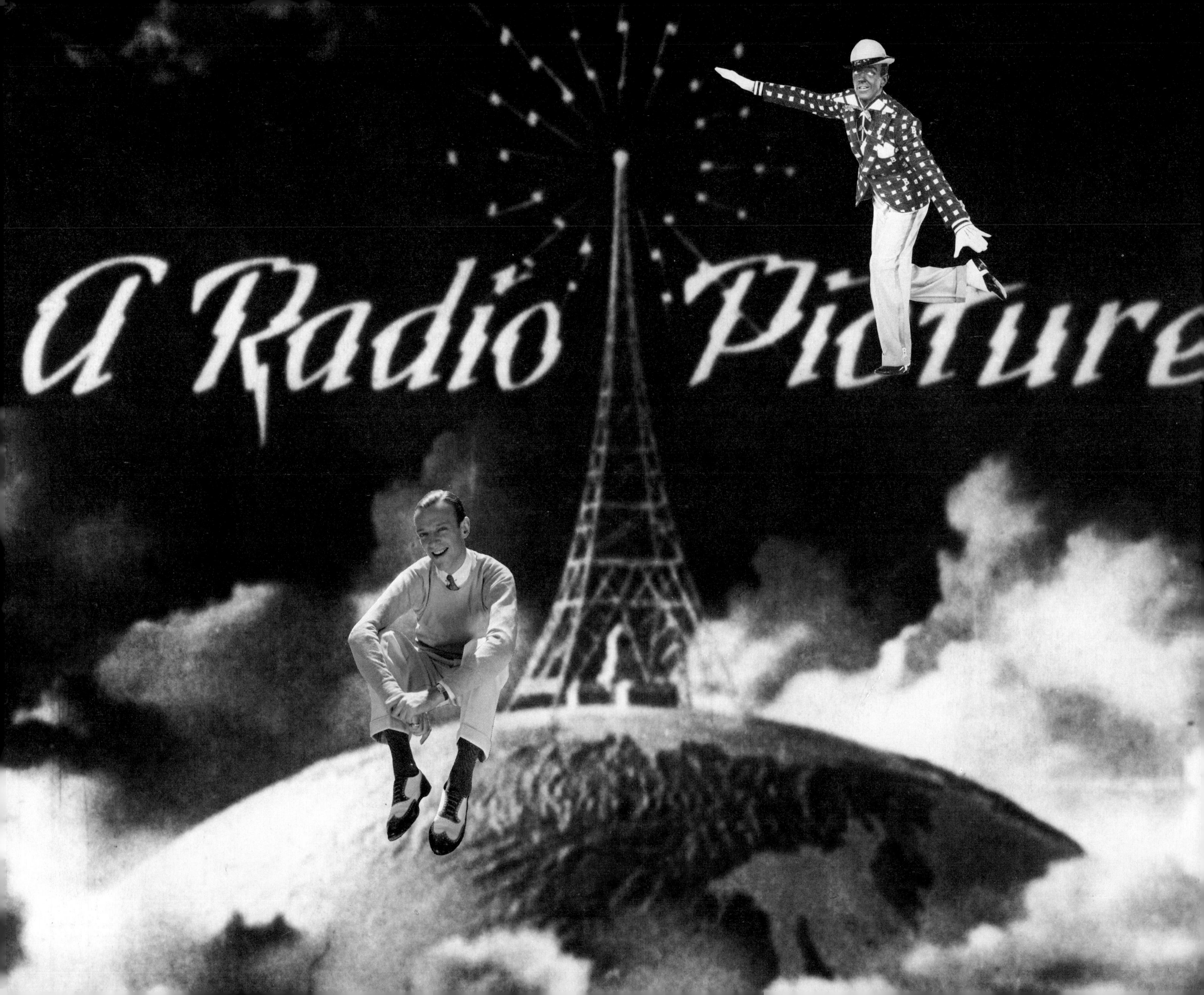
A Radio Picture

For Lester —
Best from —
Fred Astaire
'80

Opposite page: *The "Radio Pictures" logo (c. 1932). Shortly after the Astaire–Ginger Rogers cycle of musicals began in December of 1933, this logo was changed to read "An RKO Radio Picture." Fred, in blackface, performing the "Bojangles of Harlem" number in the film* Swingtime *(1936).* This page: *A theater lobby card for* Swingtime *(1936). A publicity photograph from* Top Hat *(1935).*

Military motifs: Fred proved that he did not have to wear his legendary top hat, white tie, and tails to maintain his incredibly appealing and boyish nonchalance. At the onset of World War II, Columbia Pictures drafted him into the Movie Military, where he was given the chance to dance with a shimmeringly beautiful dream named Rita Hayworth. This combination created an alliance that struck sparks of lush eroticism and enchanting sexuality; You'll Never Get Rich (1941). Pre–World War II Movie Military: Fred as a sailor in Follow the Fleet (1936).

Another shipboard dance:
Shall We Dance *(1937).*
Private First Class Fred
Astaire, You'll Never Get
Rich. *For selling millions of
dollars' worth of defense
bonds, for dancing through
hundreds of USO army
camp tours, for dancing on
the backs of trucks just
behind the front lines, up
and down the aisles of
hospital wards and in
prisoner-of-war camps, Fred
was given a souvenir Iron
Cross by admiring troops.*

Finding Fred Astaire at the five-and-ten was, for some inexplicable reason, never very easy. Once in a while fate smiled on me and there appeared something as wonderful as a paper-doll cutout with him on the cover. This one featured the film Holiday Inn, Paramount Pictures (1942). A Columbia Pictures publicity photograph (c. 1942). His immortalization in the sidewalk of Hollywood Boulevard.

THANK YOU Si

Fred Astaire

FEB 4 58

The terrific "Steppin' Out With My Baby" number... Astaire at his best, Irving Berlin music, glorious Technicolor!

*T*echnicolor gave Fred Astaire a dimension that he had inexplicably lacked in some of his earlier black-and-white movies. It brought him to a new peak of perfection, something that made watching him more wonderful than a dream of walking on air. Theater lobby cards for two of his biggest M.G.M. hits, Easter Parade *(1948) and* Ziegfeld Follies *(1946).* In The Babbit and the Bromide, *Fred teamed up with Gene Kelly,* Ziegfeld Follies *(1946).*

The dates designate the year in which each photograph was taken. Left to right: Ann Miller, On the Town, M.G.M. (1949). Ann Miller, Paramount Pictures (1941). Mae West, Paramount Pictures (c. 1933).

MAE WEST

P 1446-171

Left to right: *Marlene Dietrich, "I Wish You Love," CBS-TV (1973).*
Virginia O'Brien, Ziegfeld Follies, M.G.M. (1946).
Vera Zorina, Sam Goldwyn Studios (c. 1937).

Sky-high musical show!

CABIN IN THE SKY

Go gay with this great cast!

* ETHEL WATERS
* Eddie "ROCHESTER" Anderson
* LENA HORNE
* Louis Armstrong * Rex Ingram
* Duke Ellington & His Orchestra
* The Hall Johnson Choir

To Lester, most sincerely, Lena Horne

"That's My Boy!" by VAN JOHNSON'S DAD

Modern Screen

MAY 15¢

DELL

To Lester

To Lester, Best, Gene Kelly

Left to right: *Lena Horne,
c. 1943. Van Johnson
fan magazine cover
(1942). Gene Kelly,
Tom and Jerry;* Anchors
Aweigh, *M.G.M.
(1945). June Allyson,*
Best Foot Forward,
*Broadway stage
(1941). Hope
Hampton, Universal
Pictures (c. 1936). Hedy
Lamarr, M.G.M.
(c. 1942).*

HILLARD ELKINS • MARTIN ... present

"STYLISH, FUNNY, FASCINATING, THEATRICAL! DO SEE THIS MAN!"
— Barnes, N.Y. Post

"GAIETY IN THE ORIGINAL SENSE OF THE WORD! 'QUENTIN CRISP' IS WITTY, TOUCHING, AND VERY FUNNY. HE IS THE MESSAGE IN THE BOTTLE."
— Eder, N.Y. Times

QUENTIN CRISP

ENGAGEMENT EXTENDED NOW thru FEB. 11

THE NAKED CIVIL SERVANT

THE PLAYERS THEATRE
115 MacDougal Street, N.Y.C. • (212) 254-5076

Quentin Crisp (1979). Gloria Swanson, Sunset Boulevard, Paramount Pictures (1950). Groucho Marx, CBS Radio (c. 1932).

To
Lester Glassner
My Fan
and,
Good Friend
Iris Adrian

True Experiences

The Secret Behind Their Love Story

10¢

SEPTEMBER

UNMASKED

The Story of a Prelude to Love

BOOK LENGTH TRUE NOVEL

KATHARINE ALDRIDGE

Iris Adrian, Paramount
Pictures (c. 1934).
Katherine Aldridge (c.
1939). Margaret Hamilton,
Judy Garland, The Wizard
of Oz, M.G.M. (1939).
Margaret O'Brien, M.G.M.
(c. 1944). Billie Holiday,
Columbia Records album
(c. 1956).

DIME-STORE DEFINITIONS

BAKELITE: A trademark for any of a group of thermosetting (permanent hardening or solidifying upon heating) plastics having high chemical and electrical resistance. It was used in a wide variety of manufactured objects such as toys, appliances, flooring, hardware and packaging, and was invented by Leo H. Bakeland. **CELLULOID:** A trademark for a colorless, flammable material made from nitrocellulose and camphor. It was used in the manufacturing of toys, cosmetic packaging, jewelry, and many household items. Of all the plastics made before World War II, celluloid alone presented the warm feeling of life to the touch. **TECHNICOLOR:** A trademark for a motion-picture color process in which a dye absorbed in gelatin is transferred by contact and pressure to another material (e.g., blank film). This process is known as imbibition or dye transfer (hence the designation IB Tech.), and it is used by film collectors as a universal code name for highly collectible Hollywood movies which were *designed* in color. **COMPOSITION:** Liquefied wood pulp mixed with plant fibers and hardeners. It was used in the mass production of toys, dolls, and figurines throughout the 1930s and prewar 1940s.